HESIOD AND THE LANGUAGE OF POETRY

HESIOD
AND THE LANGUAGE
OF POETRY

PIETRO PUCCI

THE JOHNS HOPKINS UNIVERSITY PRESS
Baltimore and London

This book has been brought to publication with the generous assistance of the Andrew W. Mellon Foundation.

Copyright © 1977 by The Johns Hopkins University Press

Manufactured in the United States of America

The Johns Hopkins University Press, Baltimore, Maryland 21218
The Johns Hopkins Press Ltd., London

Library of Congress Catalog Card Number 76-234
ISBN 0-8018-1787-0

Library of Congress Cataloging in Publication data
will be found on the last printed page of this book.

iv

CONTENTS

81- 0087

ACKNOWLEDGMENTS

This book was written with invaluable assistance from many sources. I wrote the first section of it when I was a fellow at the Center for Hellenic Studies in Washington, and I pursued its thesis during a sabbatical year in Rome, for which I received financial assistance from the American Council of Learned Societies. I also received generous support from Cornell Faculty Research Grants.

During and after the writing of this book I was able to discuss my views with several scholars. I thank the directors of classical institutes, conferences and seminars who invited me to present the results of my work: U. Albini (University of Genova), R. Dyer (University of Massachusetts), B. Gentili (University of Urbino), B. Knox (Center for Hellenic Studies), C. F. Russo (University of Bari), and R. Scott (Bryn Mawr); from the discussions that ensued at these meetings I reaped much useful criticism, which helped me to formulate more correctly or more precisely some of my points. I also owe thanks for useful comments from G. Kirkwood and M. Stokes, who read a draft of the first chapter. Particular thanks go to G. Nagy, a careful and supportive reader of my manuscript; his creative scholarship helped much more than the few references to his books or papers may indicate.

The critical method I follow will be manifest to the reader. The works of J. P. Vernant—with whom I discussed my interpretation of Pandora—of M. Detienne, and of J. Derrida constitute the premises of my study. Any weaknesses or misjudgments are my own.

Introduction

THE GIFTS OF THE GODS

On Mount Helikon the Muses meet Hesiod, give him the staff, and breathe into him their divine voice (*Th.* 24 ff.). Imbued with their song, Hesiod can sing about the past and the future (*Th.* 32), interpret and sing the mind of Zeus (*Erga* 661), and recount an "immense" or "divine" song (*Erga* 662); he masters the entire holy history of the gods, their origin and succession, and the history of men's past ages (*Erga* 106 ff.). Everything Hesiod sings proceeds from the truthful song of the Muses: lacking all familiarity with navigation, Hesiod still does not feel inadequate to teach it, informed as he is by the Muses (*Erga* 649 and 661 f.). Like a prophet, Hesiod speaks through the mouth of the goddesses who have selected and favored him with this gift—for their *logos* is a gift to the poets (*Th.* 103).

Wholly dependent on the inspiration of the Muses, the poet sets the very principle of his poetry at stake, for the Muses, ambiguous entities, confess their ability to tell lies that are similar or identical to truths (*Th.* 27). Hesiod, however, is convinced that such a dangerous *logos* is administered by the Muses to other poets, not to himself. He entertains this conviction with some confidence, since the Muses reveal their ambiguity or doubleness to him alone, as pupil and devotee.

This is the poet's belief. It is indeed a remarkable proof of his faith that, having exposed the doubleness of the Muses' *logos*, Hesiod feels neither excessive alarm nor wariness. Only the Muses can know if their discourse is truth or a lie disguised as truth, but Hesiod does not seem apprehensive.

Yet he should. For the reader perceives that the doubleness of the Muses' *logos* affects even the song of Hesiod; in accordance with its divine nature, the *logos,* similar to truth but different from truth, creeps into the text of the poet. It is my intention, therefore, to consider Hesiod's candid confession about the doubleness of the words of the Muses and to investigate the implications of this doubleness. I shall demonstrate that the oddity, or the paradox

1

of the *logos* of the Muses, produces further paradoxes, contradictions, doubles, polysemies, and ambiguities throughout Hesiod's text; and I shall consider these paradoxical structures as extensions of the paramount paradox of the *logos*—what is now called the paradox of writing.

In principle, I might have directed the present investigation to the entire text of Hesiod, but I have chosen to limit myself to two main figures or themes: that of Dikê (and dikê), and that of Pandora, for their signally para-doxical features are especially pronounced and exposed. It is these figures who offer the key with which to open the gate to the intricate labyrinth of their text. Pandora comprehends striking paradoxes, oddities, and contradic-tions. She is presented as an evil to be loved by men, as a piece of earth molded to resemble the goddesses, as an evil gift of Zeus that carries death to men and secures for them the continuation of their race.

The poet celebrates Dikê as a gift of Zeus (*Erga* 279-80) and, more pre-cisely, as his daughter and assistant; suddenly, Dikê's weakness and Zeus's absence shock and dismay both poet and listener.

The evident paradoxical structures of these figures were what first attracted my attention and stimulated my inquiry. And in the course of my work I have come to understand better the parallelism that can be reconstructed in Hesiod's text between these figures and the *logos* of the Muses. Like the *logos* of the Muses, which acts as a *mediator* between gods and men, revealing to them the mind of the gods, so Dikê assists men against wrong and violence, and Pandora is used by Zeus as a weapon to punish men because of Prome-theus's disloyalty. Without raising this parallelism to any declared principle, the text nevertheless elicits this analogy: Dikê and Pandora mirror, in various aspects and degrees, the paramount paradox of the *logos*. For the *logos* of the Muses is split between a nature identical to truth and a nature which contra-dicts precisely that claim of identity.

The text states this dichotomy, or split, in the most explicit way, by speaking of two different utterances. But the investigation into the causes and inner mechanics of the two aspects of the Muses' *logos* stops here. The text declares only the necessity for and the inescapability of things being as they are, and it declares this by defining the *logos* of the Muses and the two other figures as "gifts" of the gods.

A "gift" of the gods is most often an inevitability whose nature and whose necessity for man lie beyond the reach of human understanding. The point is well made by Paris, when he invites Hector to desist from his reproaches:

> Do not bring up against me the lovely gifts of Golden Aphrodite.
> For the magnificent gifts of the Gods—whatever they want to give—
> cannot be cast away, and no man by his own will would choose them.
>
> (*Il.* 3. 64-65)

The odd quality of the gift of the gods is well demonstrated by Paris: the gift is lovely (ἐρατά), but no one would choose it willingly. Furthermore, though it is a gift, it cannot be cast away. (This idea is, of course, proverbial: see *Od.* 18. 142; *Hymn. Dem.* 147-48, 216-17, Solon 13, 64, etc.). Our impression of this oddness is further reinforced if we recall that even the young and inexperienced Telemachos can refuse a gift promised to him by the famous Menelaos. Telemachos refuses on the grounds that for him, Menelaos's gift would be perfectly useless.

The odd nature of the divine gift deserves our attention because it constitutes the "mythical" foundation and explanation for both the ambiguous quality of the Muses' *logos* and for Pandora. In the case of Paris we recognize easily how, entertaining the notion of divine gift, he accommodates both the good—though uncontrollable—will of the gods and the necessity for the existence of things as they are. Yet this notion establishes more than just the peculiar qualities of a hero—his beauty, seductive power, or musical skill— with it Homer and Hesiod imply the emergence of the painful condition of mortals: both good and evil emanate from Zeus's two jars in *Il.* 24. 527 ff.; their existence is permitted by Zeus in *Od.* 6. 188 ff.; Pandora, the beginning of the human fall, is a "gift" of Zeus and of the gods (*Erga* 82, 85-86); poverty is given by Zeus (*Erga* 638) or by the gods (*Erga* 718); and, finally, the unavoidable condition of man is again a "gift" of the gods in the *Hymn. Dem.* 147 ff. We face, therefore, a "mythical" theme that traces the emergence of human misery back to a gift, that finds the "origin" of human unhappiness in a divine donation. In contrast to human gifts—which are desirable, precious, and generally dispensable—the gift of the gods assumes a curiously paradoxical quality.[1] Furthermore, it identifies the origin of the human condition not with the very existence of the world—chaos or order—but with the peculiar structure of the gift, that is, with a paradoxical addition. In fact, as we shall see, Pandora is added to the paradisiacal status of the world as an addition that destroys that status, as an excess that provokes the end of the paradise, as an acquisition that dissipates all the goods of the preexisting world. The present human condition, therefore, does not come about as the result of a *simple shift* produced by Zeus from positive to negative order, from fullness to deprivation; it ensues through a process of addition, excess, and supplementarity of which the gift is the figure and the embodiment.

The threatening power of this process can also be seen when the gift is intended as a positive and fruitful addition, as the poetic *logos* is. Suffice it here to point out that this gift of the Muses should enable the poet to recover a lost privilege, divine memory, and truth: yet it is unsolicited and uncontrollable; it can lead to truth or the worst fallacy; it establishes the origin of poetry in a territory that lies beyond the control of man.

Hesiod's reticence in speculating on the attributes of the *logos* does not prevent us from supplying a theory that might penetrate the full sense of his statement about the duplicity of the *logos* and trace the meaningful marks left by it in the text. This theory is contingent on a modern awareness that all text is fundamentally "open"—structured and made compact by conflicting or many-sided impulses. While this general statement seems acceptable to many current critics of different schools and philosophical approaches, the reader may recognize the more precise arguments for a theory of language and text as being derived from the work of Jacques Derrida.

A theory that posits the conflicting, polysemic nature of language as an inescapable reality, that declares the openness of meaning, the initial double-ness of all text, will not consider Hesiod's statement about the doubleness of the *logos* of the Muses a paradox. In fact, Hesiod's statement is a paradox only in form: Hesiod's claim that he has fully escaped the doubleness of language and his confidence in speaking the *logos* of identity with truth are the "mythi-cal" elements.

I should say a word about the use of the term *logos*. I may be criticized for using this word to indicate what Hesiod and Homer habitually call a "song"—*aoide* or *hymnos*. Nevertheless, the word is used, though rarely, in the epos. It occurs twice in Homer: *Il.* 15. 393 and *Od.* 1. 56. In the first instance, it refers to Patroclos, who is entertaining Eurypylos with tales while tending the latter's wound. Although it is difficult to detect the pre-cise connotation of the word in this passage, the connection established be-tween entertaining with *logoi* and tending a wound should not pass unnoticed:

> ἦστό τε καὶ τὸν ἔτερπε λόγοις, ἐπὶ δ' ἕλκεϊ λυγρῷ
> φάρμακ' ἀκέσματ' ἔπασσε μελαινάων ὀδυνάων.

The therapeutic nature of this *logos* has in fact been suggested by P. Lain Entralgo (*The Therapy of the Word*). In *Od.* 1. 56, on the other hand, the word *logos* seems to carry pejorative connotations: it refers to the "soft and crafty" blandishments with which Calypso tries to make Odysseus forget his home:

> αἰεὶ δὲ μαλακοῖσι καὶ αἱμυλίοισι λόγοισι
> θέλγει, ὅπως Ἰθάκης ἐπιλήσεται·

In Hesiod's *Theogony*, *logos* is personified once as the son of Eris and is included in a catalog of such evils as Strife, Falsehood, and Dispute (*Th.* 229). It means, probably, "speeches" of contention. In another passage (*Th.* 890) it carries the same somewhat negative meaning identified in *Od.* 1. 56.

In Hesiod's *Erga, logos* twice connotes wiles and lies (78 and 789) and once has the neutral sense of a "tale" (*Erga* 106). Interestingly, in this unique epic occurrence with the neutral sense of "discourse," "tale," or "narrative," *logos* designates what we moderns would call "myth."

I should probably emphasize that the distinction between *to sing* and *to tell* is not made even in the specific case of the Muses. In *Theogony* 27-28 the Muses can indifferently λέγειν and γηρύσασθαι. The difference between the two expressions probably lies only in the high style of γηρύσασθαι. But if the Muses can λέγειν, their discourse can be a λόγος.

There is, therefore, no reason to reject the word *logos* for the poetic narrative of Hesiod. The word *logos,* on the contrary, has at least two advantages. First, it is the word which means discourse, narrative, etc., throughout Greek literature. To speak of Hesiod's or Homer's *logos* implies recognition of a problem of the *logos* that transcends both the historical period of these poets and the particular nature of Hesiod's and Homer's poetic discourse. Secondly, the word *logos* is used by Hesiod to designate what we would call a "myth." One need only think of the title of Nestle's *Vom Mythos zum Logos* to realize how inaccurate the linguistic distinction between "myth" and "*logos*" is, though it has been so pervasively supported for Homer and Hesiod. The use of the word *logos* for the entire discourse of Hesiod, therefore, implies a recasting of the question, "What is myth?" In the course of this analysis the reader will find some suggestions for the rethinking of this problem.

*Except when it is otherwise indicated, I quote Hesiod from the following texts:

Hesiod. *Theogony.* Edited with prolegomena and commentary by M. L. West. Oxford, 1966. (Cited as West.)
Hesiod. *Opera et dies.* Recensuit A. Colonna. Milan, 1959. (Cited as Colonna.)

Translations are mine, unless otherwise indicated.

NOTES

1.   Often in Homer's and Hesiod's poems the gifts of the gods (δῶρα θεῶν) appear as divine goods, favors, and privileges. Thus, the gods are "donors of

goods" in general (*Od.* 8. 325; Hes. *Th.* 46—in an epithetic expression). The horses of Achilles (*Il.* 16. 381, etc.), his armor (*Il.* 18. 84, etc.), the garden of Alcinous (*Od.* 7. 132), etc., are examples of such gifts. But such favors and privileges are more often mentioned as emanating from an individual god: thus, for instance, Paris, before generalizing on the gifts of the gods, defines his own charms as gifts of Aphrodite (*Il.* 3. 54, 64)—and sexual pleasure is often defined as such: see *Aspis* 47, *Hymn. Dem.* 102. Analogously, wine is defined as a gift of Dionysos (*Erga* 614); the bow as a gift of Apollo (*Il.* 2. 827); and the arts are gifts of Athena (*Od.* 7. 110 f.); fire is a gift of Zeus (Hes. *Th.* 563).

HESIOD AND THE LANGUAGE OF POETRY

Chapter 1

THE TRUE AND FALSE DISCOURSE IN HESIOD

> . . . thou art no slave
> Of that false secondary power, by which,
> In weakness, we create distinctions, then
> Deem that our puny boundaries are things
> Which we perceive, and not which we have made.
> Wordsworth, *The Prelude*
> (1805 version)

THE LOGOS AS IMITATION AND DIFFERENCE

One of the striking novelties of Hesiod's work is his literary self-awareness as a poet and, more specifically, his elaboration of puzzling and odd views about his art, poetic song, or discourse.[1] The purpose of this chapter is to investigate Hesiod's text as it explores the complex, puzzling nature of poetic discourse. As is well known, the Muses, patron goddesses of poetry, utter in the *Theogony* (26 ff.) one of the most enigmatic statements about poetry to be found in Greek literature.

We begin our analysis with a discussion of Zeus and the Muses, both of whom appear so emphatically at the beginning of the *Erga* and the *Theogony*. In a passage of the *Erga*, Hesiod maintains that the right time for sowing is the fall and that if grain is sown at the winter solstice it will suffer from the dry weather. Yet there are exceptional cases when late sowing might be good, for the mind of Zeus is inscrutable and it changes at every moment (483–84).[2] Though Zeus's inscrutability is a conventional trait of the god,[3] his inconsistency ("sometimes he is of one mind, sometimes of another mind" [483]) reveals a less familiar characteristic. To be sure, Zeus's changes of mind are evident not in his words but in the events of nature. Yet his ambiguity parallels that of the Muses, who are his daughters and Hesiod's teachers.[4] (Δί'

8

ἐννέπετε σφέτερον πατέρ᾿ [*Erga* 2])
   When the Muses meet Hesiod on Mount Helikon they tell him

> "ποιμένες ἄγραυλοι, κάκ᾿ ἐλέγχεα, γαστέρες οἶον,
> ἴδμεν ψεύδεα πολλὰ λέγειν ἐτύμοισιν ὁμοῖα,
> ἴδμεν δ᾿ εὖτ᾿ ἐθέλωμεν ἀληθέα γηρύσασθαι."

(*Th.* 26 ff.)

"Shepherds of the fields, poor fools, mere bellies!
We know how to say many lies similar [or identical]
to true things, but if we want, we know how to
sing the truth."

The strong assonance—almost an anagram or a reverse reading—of *ethelō-*(*men*) and *alethea* emphasizes the explicit statement that truth depends only on the wish of the Muses; the Muses often tell lies that look like truths.[5] To be sure, there is a distinction between lies and truth: lies that look like truth are prosaically and simply "said" (λέγειν), while truth that is really truth is qualified by a verb from religious language (γηρύσασθαι) and seems to merit a higher tone. But this distinction is only a matter of emphasis rather than a substantial difference.[6] The puzzling statement hides a deeper distinction: leaving aside the religious significance of the Muses' statement (see Detienne, pp. 75 ff.), I should like to open a discussion of its linguistic significance.

It is remarkable that Hesiod, the supposedly mythical thinker, should, first, deny "the Homeric belief in the identity of truth and poetry" (Luther, p. 42) and, second, represent the relationship between truth and falsehood in rationalistic terms. In stating that the untrue statements of the Muses look like truth Hesiod evokes the concept of *imitation*, which is fundamental to Greek thought on language. The precise meaning of this text has never—to my knowledge—been elucidated: what is it that is imitated by the false statements of the Muses (ψεύδεα—from ψεῦδος—λέγειν)? Given that ὁμοῖος can suggest both similarity and identity,[7] what precise relationship is established between the true and the untrue? The word ἔτυμα (i.e., the truth that the false statements of the Muses imitate) might mean both that which actually exists and that which is thought or said to be true.[8] But, since ἔτυμος has a positive formation and is possibly connected with εἶναι, one might wish here to stress its meaning as "what actually exists as true."[9] The text of line 27 would then imply that the Muses' false *logos* (ψεύδεα λέγειν) resembles things that exist or have happened. If line 27 echoes *Odyssey* 19. 203, where the author comments on Odysseus's ability to invent fictitious facts about himself, the passage of the *Theogony* might suggest that the Muses invent stories which are similar or even identical to actual facts or events. But we should not ignore

the differences between the respective implications of the two passages: whereas the inventions of Odysseus are mere expedients, tactical moves of common
language, the *logos* of the Muses constitutes the divine "gift" of poetry. Their
definition of the *logos* as something "tricky" bears on the language of all poetry. Furthermore, since the *locus* of truth lies in the things and the events themselves, Odysseus's stories are subject to verification by a search of evidences and
witnesses; but the Muses' song about the past and the future lies beyond the
limits of any inquiry. The poor shepherds whom the Muses address are deceived
by the plausibility of their words, just as Penelope is deceived by the words of
Odysseus. Within our established context, these poor shepherds represent all
poets—their wisdom, memory, and truth—before Hesiod.

We should now explore the larger implications of a principle which holds
that words are similar or identical to true things. From the position taken in
line 27 it follows that the *logos* is at once similar to and different from truth; the
logos imitates things, but it does so always with some distortion. This duplicity
becomes more apparent in an analysis of the Homeric expressions that indicate
"lie" and "truth." The terms in question always imply a relation of imitation
or closeness between words and real things, events, or ideas. In *Od.* 4. 347 f.
Menelaos assures Telemachos that he is speaking the truth:

> ταῦτα δ᾽ ἅ μ᾽ εἰρωτᾷς καὶ λίσσεαι, οὐκ ἄν ἐγώ γε
> ἄλλα παρὲξ εἴποιμι παρακλιδόν, οὐδ ἀπατήσω·

LSJ (s.v. παρακλιδόν) translates, "I would not tell you another tale beside the
mark and swerving *from the truth*," but the words "mark" and "truth" are
not in the Greek. A more precise rendering would be, "I would not say other
things beside [what I heard from the truthful old man] and obliquely [i.e.,
deviating from what the same person told me]." Menelaos means, therefore,
that he will *repeat* the words he has heard without deflection and *mirror*
them[10] without difference. As we have already seen in *Od.* 19. 203, in another
instance, Odysseus invents a false story whose credibility lies in its similarity
to possible true events; in fact, his story is a mixture of half-truths.

This interpretation is confirmed by an analysis of the Greek expressions
meaning "truth": they aim at the things themselves as they are. Thus, for
instance, the expression ἀτρεκέως καταλέγειν implies a *logos* without distortion or deflection (see W. Luther, *Wahrheit und Lüge*, pp. 42–50), as indicated by the negative composition of ἀ–*τρέκος (cf. the Latin *torqueo*).
Moreover, νημερτής, meaning "who does not miss the goal" (Luther, "Wahrheit Licht" pp. 33–43), implies a *logos* hitting things or going straight to
them. And the case of ἀλήθεια is well known (see notes 42 and 43).

Given this analysis in addition to the text of *Th.* 27, the conclusion we
must stress is that the Muses sing a discourse similar to true things, but with

some distortion, invention, or deflection—in a word, with some difference. The similarity vouches for the credibility of the discourse, while the invention, deflection, and difference make it false. Moreover, the difference is of such nature that only the Muses can see it or read it. In fact, the Muses reveal this difference to Hesiod for the first time, and by declaring what *had escaped* men in the Muses' song, they reveal the *a-letheia* (28). This interpretation would justify the meaning of ὁμοῖα as "identical," at least from the point of view of the shepherds, since for them there is really no difference between the song of the Muses and the ἔτυμα.[11] For these shepherds—and, with them, all of epic culture—see, in the *logos* of the Muses, no distortion, no deviation from reality. There is no way they can have seen it: if they had sensed the difference, they would not have accepted the *logos* of the Muses as identical to true things.

In the face of the surreptitious power of the *logos* the impotence of man is demonstrated clearly: only the Muses can see beyond the magic mirror of *logos*. (I disregard the question of whether the *logos* is in rapport with things themselves or with their image in our mind,[12] which is a question that is impossible for our text to resolve and that troubled Aristotle.[13])

The same conclusions are reached if we interpret the text of *Theogony* 27 to mean "we know how to say an untrue *logos* similar/identical to a true one." With this reading, the relationship between words and things is replaced by a relationship between two meanings of the same *logos*. This interpretation is improbable in our context, but let us pursue it briefly, as it is supported by the analogy to various words in the *Erga*, each of which evokes different or even opposite connotations for single persons or entities. The name "Eris," for instance, means both a good and a bad Eris (*Erga* 11 ff.). In fact, the text implies that the word "Eris" evokes two persons at once: Competition, to be praised, and Discord, to be blamed. The word "Eris" functions as the sign for a double: it means at once two opposite persons. Analogously, when Hesiod speaks of a bad *Aidos* (*Erga* 315 ff.), he implies the existence of a good one; similarly, he speaks of a day (*Hemere*, *Erga* 825) that is viewed either as a mother or a stepmother. Here again, the same word conjures up a double image and implies two opposite persons or qualities. Though the complex relationship between name and *logos* is not easy to define, one might be tempted to extend the ambivalence of the name to the paradox of line 27. The *logos* of the Muses, in this case, would not connote a good and a bad entity, but would express a true and a false statement. More precisely, the Muses would claim that their *logos*, though it repeats a true one, is untrue. Though the Muses establish a relationship of similarity/identity between two meanings, they are able to distinguish the original (truth) from its copy (falsehood). This proposition raises some hair-splitting questions, for it introduces

the difficult problem of assessing the relationship between copy and model
and of discerning the elements that mark the model, or original. In particular,
if we assume ὁμοῖα to mean "identical," the result is the paradox of a lie that
is identical to truth and yet is falsely recognizable as a truth. In this case of
perfect homonymy, not even the Muses would be able to read the difference;
moreover, a language formed by total homonymy, (i.e., without any difference at all), would not be language, because it would lack the distinctive and
differential marks that generate meaning. If we allow that some distinctive and
differential marks exist, only the Muses might read them, for the distinctive
marks of the *logos* do not reveal to man a sufficient difference between truth
and falsehood.

As indicated above, we have pursued this argument because of the homonymies that Hesiod is fond of introducing into his text. Yet, as we shall see,
the false *logos* is in fact different from the things it evokes, and not from a
truthful *logos*. This interpretation should therefore be set aside, although
the presence of perfect homonymies might well undermine Hesiod's confidence that the Muses speak to him a discourse *identical* to "the things as they
are" (ἔτυμα).

We may conclude that the *logos* signifies things by *imitating* them with
some obliquity, distortion, and addition. Nevertheless, this difference, this
movement askance, is not perceptible to men, as only the Muses recognize it.
However, before we examine why only the Muses can fathom the difference,
let us recapitulate the predicament of the poet.

The insults that the Muses address to the shepherds should be understood
as a strong indictment of the powerlessness and ignorance of men before the
poetic *logos*. The mystery of the *logos* is no wonder; for the *logos* is a gift
of the gods. Not all song, even that produced by the Muses, is true; nevertheless, sung in the voice of the Muses, it always appears as truth. This dis-
heartening message leaves the poet alone, facing the precariousness of the
logos. As Hesiod (still often considered to have been on the threshold of
mythical thinking), begins a new type of song, he boldly accepts his own
individual responsibility for truth; and with tremendous energy he denies
the general demonstrability of truth.

Yet Hesiod's responsibility for truth implies a faith in the Muses' wish to
tell him the truth. As indicated above, the text of line 28 ("we know, when
we want, how to sing true things") locates the power of saying the truth in
the Muses' will: the difference of the *logos* from the "things as they are" is
not a necessary condition of every *logos* but a condition contingent on the
capricious will of the Muses.

It is not difficult to understand why the Muses constitute the unique *locus* of truth for the poet, why only they know whether or not their song is
truthful. According to *Il.* 2. 485 ff., the Muses alone are beholders of the

events that the poet celebrates. They are, as goddesses, the only witnesses of the past events whose narration they inspire in the poet. This conception is conventional and crosses the entire classical tradition: *Th.* 30–34, Gorg. *Hel.* 2, Ap. Rhod. *Argon.* 4. 1379 f., Verg. *Aen.* 9. 77 ff., etc.[14]

The poet, therefore, does not personally have any direct knowledge of that which he sings: like Penelope in *Od.* 19, who cannot discern those lies of Odysseus that are similar to truth, he is powerless to verify the song of the Muses. Hesiod celebrates "the past and the future" (*Th.* 32), and he evidently must rely on the Muses' account.

We can now better comprehend the powerful description of his encounter with the Muses: using epic machinery to dramatize the encounter with a god, the poet attributes the force of reality to the Muses' trustworthiness and willingness to speak the truth.

Since the Muses are the only source of truth, and since the poet will forever be unable to compare their song with "the things as they are," he *cannot* be aware of the distortions, deflections, and inventions that draw the poetic discourse into falsehood and fiction. We are brought back to our initial concern. Within the general notion of language as imitation, Hesiod's text raises troubling questions. First, if, as we have maintained, the very presence of the things as they are is always missing, and if language is imitation (i.e., simulation of identity), then the poet is doomed to blindness with regard to the truth of his own song.[15] Second, and more distressingly, the notion of imitation imperils the very possibility of representing truth. Any imitation implies by definition a difference from the original or the model, since without this difference, imitation would cease being imitation and would become identity. Therefore, imitation must appear always as a simulation of identity, of originality. In other words, imitation always implies that minimal distortion and deflection which make discourse false.

Here we may perceive how the text overcomes this difficulty: by exploiting the ambiguity of the word ὁμοῖα, which implies both similarity and identity, Hesiod, in line 28, suggests (as we shall soon see) that the song the Muses sing to him is in fact identical to truth.

Finally, since the *locus* of truth (i.e., the very presence of the things as they are) is always missing, truth is contained only within the *logos*; it appears only in the form of imitation of or identity with this absent truth. This means that truth can be recovered only by and through the *logos* itself: the presence of things as they are does not manifest itself in any other way than as dubbing, imitation, or representation. The "original" signified is always absent. Truth is always, therefore, only "inscription" of the *logos*, in the sense that truth (i.e., things as they are) is aimed at through the movement of the *logos* in the act of writing off its difference and deferral. Through this metaphor of "inscription" I am referring to Derrida's insight that the *logos* should be viewed as a protowriting (*archiécriture*), i.e., as a differential and deferring structure. The "signified" is always caught in the web of the differential, deferring, negative relationships that allow the emergence of meaning, and can never appear as present, *hic et nunc*.

Though we cannot say to what extent Hesiod is aware of these problems, they are certainly raised by his text. At any rate, he overcomes the problem implicit in the notion of imitation as difference from the original by stating in line 28 that the Muses can sing the truth. The perplexing question of ὁμοῖα finds a solution of some sort: in view of line 27 we have to understand that the Muses sing a song without difference from truth and *identical* to it.

Hesiod, then, avoids the problems his text raises. Whether imitation always implies some difference, whether the simulation of identity may always go undetected, whether truth is always only inscription of the *logos*—these are questions that he removes by affirming a song *identical* to truth.

Even at this early juncture one can recognize that Hesiod's implicit view of language is by no means less complex than the view developed in later Greek thought. On the contrary, we perceive in Hesiod's text the contradiction that dominates later Greek thought: the contradiction between the view of language as an entity independent of external reality (language as difference—ἕτερον, as Gorgias writes—from the things, the ὄντα) and the view of language that interprets imitation of things/notions as the means of truthful discourse. While the former view can be approximately identified with the sophistic theory of language, the latter represents the goal toward which both Plato and Aristotle, in their different ways, tend. But even a cursory outline of these theories will show that the contradiction—expressed though not elaborated in Hesiod's text—is never really resolved and that it haunts all thinkers or poets.

In the *Hippolytus* (385–86) of Euripides, Phaedra remarks that the same word, *aidos*, can be used to imply either a good or a bad attitude of respect; she deduces that the ambiguity of meaning must mirror some ambiguity in the concept itself. Were *aidos* two different and distinctive entities, there would be two different words. The implication here is that language ought to mirror, and normally does mirror, the world of things and notions. On the other hand, the difference of language, the undemonstrability of language as truth or falsehood, haunts other Euripidean characters. In the same play (925 ff.) Theseus expresses the utopian dream that all men should have two voices: the usual voice, and a just and honest one added to the usual voice, "so that the dishonest voice might be refuted by the honest one and we might escape deception." Theseus is painfully aware that language does not carry any evidence of truth; trapped between two contradictory statements, he then errs with respect to both by following the direction of his own desire. Further, in the *Phoenissae* Euripides presents two characters, each of whom

prefaces his statements with an elaborate view of language and truth. Eteo-
cles asserts that the meaning of any word is ambiguous and is different for
different people (499 ff.), but Polyneices maintains, on the contrary, that a
discourse of truth is marked by certain characteristics—precision, simplicity,
lack of subtle explanation, and καιρός (469 ff.).[16]

The independence of language from the external world, its inability to mirror the world as it is, its conventional quality, and the trap that it constitutes
for logic and for truth are common themes of the sophistic theory of language.[17] But as Aristotle argues (*Met.* 1006A 12 ff.), a radical application of
these themes leads to the non-sense of talking, or speaking.

To assess the force of the reaction against the Sophists, we need only recall
one of the theses expounded in the *Cratylus*: words are naturally right since
there is correspondence between things and words. The clash between language as distortion and language as mirror haunts Plato, too. Through the complex strategy of the *Phaedrus.* Plato ascribes the sophistic attributes of the
logos to the "written" logos; he is thus able to preserve the power of mirroring truth for the spoken *logos.*[18] This strategy, which allows Plato to dispose
of the difference and deflection of the *logos* as a sophistic aspect of language,
only serves to emphasize the permanence and seriousness of the problem.
These few hints are sufficient to show that Hesiod's posture is by no means
primitive; rather, it reflects a problem that can be found in the works of
later thinkers. Though the question will receive more elaborate and more
complex answers, it continues to haunt Aristotle and the whole of Western
philosophy.[19]

If it were possible to give a superficial summary of this broad question, we
might say that the whole of our culture has conceived of language as a peculiar
medium. Though we have long been aware that language constitutes a system
of arbitrary signs relating to a referent (used here to mean both the thing and
its conceptual image), it has been tacitly assumed that we recover the referent
as it is. As though the signifier were only a screen that disappears as soon as it
indicates the signified, language has been taken as a medium that takes us to
the referent and recovers it *hic et nunc.* The sign—its differential nature, its
temporalization, its spacing—then intrudes no longer in this reappropriation
of the "thing" or of the "conceptual image."

The shattering and deconstruction of this metaphysical conception of
language have occurred in various degrees in certain periods of our intellectual history, but they have become profoundly radical and systematic in recent years, especially as a result of the work of Jacques Derrida.[20] This investigation will systematically demonstrate the impact of his philosophical
strategy.

Some readers may contend that the critic who applies modern linguistic
philosophy to the text of an ancient author like Hesiod commits a certain

violence. Certainly Hesiod has no theoretical sense of signifiers, signifieds, ref-
erents, difference, or deferral. In fact, however, we are inflicting no greater violence than any reading and interpretation must by definition inflict. We have
uncovered the tenets that hold together Hesiod's reflection upon the *logos* of
the Muses and we have discovered that a notion of imitation (ὁμοῖον) is crucial to his text. The very fecundity of our investigation may be defense
enough for the importance we accord to such a notion, along with historical
and theoretical arguments. We have considered the difficulties inherent in
this concept and have witnessed the way Hesiod sets out to overcome these
difficulties. We have unraveled the threads that hold together Hesiod's text
and that make intelligible the force of his operation. Certainly when Hesiod
speaks of a similarity between the false discourse of the Muses and truth he
implies a distortion, a deviation. We have denoted this distortion, invention,
and deflection by the word "difference," and thus far we have used the word
in its usual meaning; but we will show that this "difference" operates in the
text as "difference and deferral" in the special sense elaborated by Derrida.
We have already hinted at this sense when we demonstrated that Hesiod's
statement implies the absence of an "original" signified. Truth, which according to Hesiod should be the source of his song, appears in reality to be wholly
contained within his *logos*, inscribed in it: it is like a dubbing without original
sound track, like an imitation of that which is forever absent, like a simulation
of an "original."

If, then, the source is not a source, but rather a hypostatization of the
logos in the act of repressing its own difference, this difference—as imitation—
is the "matrix" of the concept of both true and false discourse. The concept
of false discourse derives from the idea of imitation as *difference* from things,
simulation of identity with things; the concept of true discourse also derives
from the idea of imitation, but in this case the imitation should involve no
difference. By repressing the difference, the *logos* invents its own identity
with things—the things being, as we know, ever absent and manifest only as
inscribed in the *logos*.

In the following pages we shall continue to comment on Hesiod's statements on his own *logos* and on the *logos* of the Muses. We shall trace the
series of metaphors that Hesiod invokes to illustrate the "straightness" and
steadfastness of the discourse-identical-to-truth and the "crookedness" of
its opposite.

THE STRAIGHT LOGOS

The proposition that "Truth looks similar/identical to falsehood" is replaced in line 28 by the idea that "truth" is opposed to "falsehood;" and

in the *Theogony* and *Erga*, the *logos* tends to be consistently recognizable and definable as either straight or crooked, just or unjust, unerring or erring.

We begin with the most pervasive polarity of Hesiod's *Erga*: *straight* and *crooked*. The connection between straight and true speech is implicitly made in *Theogony* 85-86, when the king, reaching a *straight* decision, is said to speak ἀσφαλέος, which is, literally, "[standing] without stumbling" and, metaphorically, "unerringly."[21] The connection between the straight and the true is further supported by the fact that it is the Muses themselves who inspire the good king to pronounce straight decisions (*Th.* 81 ff.). This connection does not imply an identity between the two values, but simply a correspondence: truth is to straightness as falsehood is to crookedness.[22] Let us add that in Homer the expression παρακλιδόν ("obliquely") is also used (*Od.* 4. 348; 7. 139) with the implicit notion of "diverting from truth."

I will comment briefly on two passages. The first one concerns the good king who is inspired by the Muses[23] and is able to reach good, just, i.e., *straight* decisions:

> διακρίνοντα θέμιστας
> ἰθείῃσι δίκῃσιν
> (*Th.* 85-86)
> settling disputes with straight decisions.

This good king speaks unerringly, and with his wisdom he stops "even a serious quarrel" (*Th.* 87). The reason that "there are good, sensitive kings,"[24] Hesiod goes on to say, is that they are able to establish justice with these qualities:

> τούνεκα γὰρ βασιλῆες ἐχέφρονες, οὕνεκα λαοῖς
> βλαπτομένοις ἀγορῆφι μετάτροπα ἔργα τελεῦσι
> ῥηιδίως, μαλακοῖσι παραιφάμενοι ἐπέεσσιν·
> (*Th.* 88-90)

> [They] obtain easily a restitution[25] for the people who
> have been wronged in their dealings,[26]
> persuading [the wrongdoers] with soft words.[27]

We have translated, following the suggestions of dictionaries and commentators, according to the sense that Hesiod obviously meant to convey; but the word for "persuading," παραιφάμενοι, means literally "to speak to deflect," "to 'de-viate' someone." The idea of persuasion in Homeric Greek is often expressed by words connoting an act of deflection, bending the mind or will of others. In *Il.* 2. 14 this notion is expressed by a verb that literally means "to bend": ἐπέγναμψεν γὰρ ἅπαντας. The implication of the idea of persuasion, therefore, is "to move the others from the path of their minds." and it focuses on the power of bending and deflecting rather than on an overriding concern for truth. In the Hesiodic passage, as we shall see, the "softness" of the words (μαλακοῖσι . . . ἐπέεσσιν) hints at some softening of truth. Moreover, the deflecting *logos* of persuasion expressed by παράφημι and πάρφασις is often used by Homer to imply the leading astray of someone by deception and deviousness.28 Strange *logos*, then, that of the good basileus! It stands firm and straight, but it constitutes a deflecting speech. The metaphor implicit in παράφημι suggests that while Hesiod praises the straightness and firmness of the right *logos*, he actually conjures up the image of "deflection" and even of "deviousness." This contradiction would be explicit enough even if we did not notice another slight incongruity in the words μετάτροπα ἔργα (89), signifying "restitution": the restitution obtained by a "straight" *logos* literally means "something which is turning back."

Our second example confirms this point. The Muses, Hesiod continues, give benefit to kings although kings are protected by Zeus, but they especially protect the poets (*Th.* 94 ff.). Fortunate the man whom the Muses love: his voice is sweet, like honey.

> When a man feels a new anguish in his grieving heart,
> and he is dried up inside from griefs, if the poet,
> servant of the Muses, sings about the glory (κλεῖα)
> of the old generations of men and about the blessed
> gods in the Olympus, that man soon forgets (ἐπιλήθεται)
> his grave thoughts, and he does not remember his
> griefs at all. And quickly the gifts of the goddesses
> (δῶρα θεάων) turn him away (παρέτραπε) from them.
>   (98-103)

The Muses can speak the truth; they inspire the words of the king who speaks unerringly and reaches *straight* decisions. They are the daughters of Zeus who straightens what is crooked (*Erga* 7); and they inspire the poets—particularly Hesiod, whom they teach on Helikon. Yet the poet, singing under their inspiration, diverts (παρέτραπε [103]) the minds of his listeners. The word παρέτραπε recalls παραιφάμενοι, the "diverting" persuasion of the good kings (*Th.* 90).29 The song of the poet, therefore, also constitutes a vehicle of diversion and has the power of leading feelings astray.

The diverting power of the *logos* is expressed by a simple concrete image, but does not lack rigor. The Muses who teach Hesiod the straight and true discourse cannot even be described without risk of imperiling their very attributes of straightness and truthfulness. For the text of the *Theogony*, immediately after lines 27-28, defines them as ἀρτιέπειαι ("glib of tongue" [*Th.* 29]). It is as if Hesiod (or his text) has taken revenge on the Muses for their *glibness* of tongue in the previous statement. Ἀρτιεπής is a *hapax* in

the epos and is used there by Hektor against Achilles to accuse him of being
"glib of tongue" and falsely boastful:

ἀλλά τις ἀρτιεπὴς καὶ ἐπίκλοπος ἔπλεο μύθων.

(Il. 22. 281)

In fact Achilles was neither glib of tongue nor bragging at the time, as the
action then shows, but this detail simply complicates the structure of reference. It is difficult to know what to make of an isolated word like this when
it is not incorporated in a formulaic expression: Hesiod might have created
the adjective independent of Homer and attributed to it the meaning of
"sound in speech" (see ἄρτια βάζειν [Il. 14. 92; Od. 8. 240]).[30]

However, the *logos* not only constitutes a sort of magic, bending power
as a gift of the goddess, but it is also described as honey. For Hesiod, speech
is like honey when spoken by either the good king who deflects the wrongdoer or the poet who turns away men's grief.[31] But if the *logos*—independent
of both the speaker and its own meaning—is like honey, it must still be different from that which it says. Some of the stories found in the honeylike
song of Muses (see *Th.* 96-97) in the *Theogony* are bitter and ominous for
mortals—e.g., the mention of Pandora's and Prometheus's story—but the
sweetness of the *logos* remains, in Hesiod's words, the same. The *logos*, therefore, derives its positive qualities—persuasiveness and healing force—from the
difference that separates it from its own meaning or content. The vicarious,
rhetorical, supplementary nature of the *logos*, a nature which evidently imperils the *logos'* ability to be at one with the truth, is here clearly suggested;
in fact, in the *Odyssey*, "to sweeten" is already a metaphor for the "distortion of truth."[32]

Since the image of honey occupies a delicate strategic position in Hesiod's
text, it merits further analysis. Both the mouth of the king (*Th.* 83-84) and
the mouth of the poet (*Th.* 97) are metaphorically represented as vessels full
of honey or as beehives from which honey pours. Far from manifesting itself
as the incorporeal breath of the Muses, poetry is characterized metaphorically
as possessing a liquid, viscous quality. This liquid, viscous matter is part of a
complex and intriguing pattern of symbolism in Homer and Hesiod which
evokes truth and the distortion of truth, oracular power and forgetfulness,
life and death.[33]

It has already been pointed out that in Homer the verb "to sweeten" implies a distortion of truth. In general, then, "honeylike" words may be said to
evoke various shades of persuasive rhetoric, from the simple desire to convince,
to the less innocent desire to deceive. It would be impossible to analyze here
all the passages in which the expression "honeylike words" appears; however,
some examples can be given. While on several occasions the epithet rings flat

and clichéd, on others it serves to emphasize the emergence of second thoughts, of scheming, of deception. Odysseus and Penelope are the paramount examples of this sweet rhetoric, since both often speak with some gain or deception in view.[34] Thus, for instance, the poet summarizes the thoughts that have gone through Odysseus's mind when the hero confronts Nausicaa:

αὐτίκα μειλίχιον καὶ κερδαλέον φάτο μῦθον
                                                    (*Od.* 6. 148)
he, on the spot, spoke honeylike and gain-seeking
words

Similarly, Penelope, much to the delight of Odysseus, addresses sweet words to the suitors with the intention of fooling them: "and . . . Odysseus rejoiced that she was trying to get gifts out of the suitors and charmed (θέλγε) their hearts with honeylike words; but her mind thought differently (ἄλλα)" (*Od.* 18. 281–83). Using the *hapax* μειλιχίη as a noun (honey-sweetness) Hesiod lists it as one of the attributes of Aphrodite, along with "maidens' whispering, smiles, deceits, sweet pleasure, and love" (*Th.* 205–6). The precise meaning of this abstract noun—whether sexual pleasure, seductive charm, or graciousness—is not easy to determine, but it obviously belongs to a semantic field that borders not on "truth" but on its opposite.

Honey, with its sticky, viscous consistency, nevertheless also symbolizes truth in general and divine truth in particular. In the *Hymn. Herm.* (558 ff.) we read of the three maiden sisters, closely associated with bees,[35] who, feeding on honeycomb, bring all things to pass: "and when they are inspired by eating blond honey they are ready and willing to speak truth (ἐθέλουσιν ἀληθείην ἀγορεύειν [561]) but if they are deprived of the sweet food of the gods they lie (ψεύδονται). . ." Hesiod's assertion that the Muses' song is truthful and sweet may well be grounded on this belief, or may at least derive its internal congruence from this association of honey with oracular truth.

This quotation is a further example of the association of truth with memory, since oracular truth and the divine song of the Muses, as we shall see, imply divine memory. Accordingly, for the same reasons that the honey-sweetness of words may be a source of deception, honey may also invoke those charms and seductions that induce forgetfulness. Suffice it to recall the epithets μείλιχος ("honeylike"), and μελίφρων ("sweet to the mind"): the former—with its synonyms—in epic poetry often qualifies various states in which honeylike words are meant to provoke forgetfulness;[36] the latter is often an epithet of wine and sleep.

The series of the oppositions hinged on the image of honey extends to a larger semantic field than hitherto suggested, when we recognize that honey also hints at a divine presence and power. It is, in fact, a variety of divine nourishment often confused with nectar, and we see that the gods also offer it as food (*Od.* 10. 234; 20. 69). As a "natural" divine food, honey symbolizes the "plenty without toil" of the golden age; in *Erga* 233, the sense of abundance is evoked by an oak tree full of acorns on the top and honey in the middle. As will become more apparent, the spontaneous plenty of nature implies a return to an innocent age, untouched by evil, falsehood, simulation, and violence. In the quoted passage, then, honey functions within the semantic field that, through the presence of the divine, implies truth, serenity, sweetness, abundance, and a sure contact with the gods.

In a rather different context, honey is associated in Homer with funeral rites (*Il.* 23. 170; *Od.* 24. 68), figuring in these passages as a remnant of the old method of embalming to preserve the dead. Thus, because of its power to preserve and restore, honey becomes further associated with death, and the vitality of this association is reinforced by later texts.[37]

It should now be evident that all the conflicting attributes of honey are also the attributes of poetry, which we have been decoding in Hesiod's text. For, like honey, the poetic *logos* implies at once the contradictory presence of divine truth and the simulation of truth, the straightness of discourse that goes directly to "things as they are" and the deflecting, intoxicating power of the word. And just as sweet sleep is related to death, so the poetic discourse, sweetening truth and inducing oblivion, is in some way akin to death.

The importance of the "honey" metaphor derives from the ambiguousness or ambivalence that it suggests in Hesiod's text. Though obviously invoked as a symbol of truth, honey, in the persuasive speech of the king or in the healing song of the poet, also evokes the softening of truth and the emergence of oblivion.

The image, therefore, can be considered to be the figurative counterpart of the concept of imitation: just as this concept holds—so to speak—the position of "matrix" in all the oppositions of truth versus falsehood, straightness versus crookedness, memory versus oblivion, and so on, so too does the image of honey lie behind all these oppositions, representing all sides simultaneously. However, while in the former case the text neatly separates imitation as simulation of identity from imitation as identity, in the latter, the text seems to harbor no suspicion of conflict, and it allows the implied incongruities to pass, as it were, unaware.

The incongruity penetrates the very heart of the image, for even the sweetness of honey comes under question when the sweetly speaking Muses open their words with violent insults: "Shepherds of the fields, poor fools, mere bellies!" Here honey evokes not sweetness, but the sharp sting of the bees.

THE SONG OF MEMORY AND OF OBLIVION

In *Theogony* 51 the poet says that the song of the Muses delights (τέρπουσι) the mind of Zeus; in the case of man, the sweet song of the poet effaces one's griefs and evidently inspires joy or pleasure. Thus, Hesiod can write of the real paradox of the poetic *logos*: the Muses, daughters of Memory, bring forth forgetfulness:

> Μοῦσαι Ὀλυμπιάδες, κοῦραι Διὸς αἰγιόχοιο·
> τὰς ἐν Πιερίῃ Κρονίδῃ τέκε πατρὶ μιγεῖσα
> Μνημοσύνη, γουνοῖσιν Ἐλευθῆρος μεδέουσα,
> λησμοσύνην τε κακῶν ἄμπαυμά τε μερμηράων.
> (*Th*. 52 ff.)

> The Muses . . . whom in Pieria did Mnemosyne [i.e.,
> Memory] . . . bear in union with the Father, son of
> Kronos, to be forgetfulness of evils and rest from
> cares.

The juxtaposition of Μνημοσύνη and λησμοσύνη at the beginning of these lines is conscious and purposeful.[38] The song of the Muses conjures up the past, the present, and the future (*Th*. 38). It is, therefore, Memory; but at the same time it diverts the mind and causes forgetfulness of the self, for it is "a forgetting of ills and rest from sorrows . . ." (*Th*. 55).

The paradox in lines 52 ff. makes a point rhetorically yet is controlled by some rationale. The daughters of Memory induce a forgetfulness of ills by restoring divine memory. This statement can be supported by the analogous effect that Hesiod ascribes to the song of the poet (*Th*. 98 ff.). As soon as the poet begins to sing "about the glory of the old generations of men and about the blessed gods in Olympus, immediately that man forgets (ἐπιλήθεται) his grave thoughts and does not remember (οὐδέ . . . μέμνηται) his griefs at all." Here too, the slipping away of present ills into forgetfulness is contingent upon the poet's introduction of another memory—that of the past and of the gods. While the paradox of lines 52 ff., therefore, makes a rhetorical point about the magical, mysterious power of the Muses, it does not imply an open contradiction within the controlled and limited opposition of Hesiod's text.

Yet the text again emphasizes that the poet's song deals only with the past (or the future), when it says that the Muses inspire the poet so that he may "sing the past and the future" (*Th*. 32). The absence of the "present" is indeed shocking, especially in view of line 38 when the Muses, teachers of Hesiod, are described as singing "*present*, future and past."[39] The effacing power of the poetic *logos* is not unlike that of a pharmakon. We may recall

Helen's pharmakon, which could prevent a man from crying even if his mother and father were to die or if he were to see before him a son or a brother being killed (*Od.* 4. 221 ff.). A song with such power is indeed a way to oblivion, overlapping the self, its present, its reality.

However, one might ask whether the song of the poet does not induce a forgetfulness more generalized and more all-embracing than that which Hesiod suggests. For, though the Muses are present there, where events happen, they cannot hand down to the poet these events themselves, but only a song that "imitates" and re-presents the events. In this recording and "re-presentation," the presence of those events emerges only as concealment and oblivion of the dubbing, the repetition, the inscription. Moreover, the events of the past are retrieved through memory, a medium that always implies oblivion, since memory chooses and selects: every text, therefore, simultaneously produces memory and oblivion.

We must therefore enlarge the limited area of Hesiod's "paradox" and realize that the Muses' song is simultaneously a song of Memory and of Oblivion. Yet a whole structure of related notions and concepts sustains the view that Memory corresponds to Truth, Straightness, and Dikê while Forgetfulness corresponds to Falsehood, Crookedness, Injustice, and Death. Detienne has elaborated this correspondence in a convincing way,[40] and here I simply illustrate the passage of *Theogony* where the correspondence is clearly and directly elicited. In *Th.* 233 ff., Nereus, the good old man of the sea, is praised for his virtues:

> Νηρέα δ' ἀψευδέα καὶ ἀληθέα γείνατο Πόντος
> πρεσβύτατον παίδων· αὐτὰρ καλέουσι γέροντα,
> οὕνεκα νημερτής τε καὶ ἤπιος, οὐδὲ θεμίστων
> λήθεται, ἀλλὰ δίκαια καὶ ἤπια δήνεα οἶδεν·

And Pontos begat as the eldest of his children Nereus,
the man without lies and truthful: men call him the
Old Man for he is infallible and kind, and he does
not forget the ordinances [or the judgments] : he
knows just and kind thoughts.

Nereus's truthfulness (ἀληθέα) is connected, among other things, with the fact that "he does not forget the ordinances [or the judgments] " (οὐδὲ θεμίστων λήθεται).[41] M. L. West (p. 233), while calling attention to line 235, develops the argument that Nereus's ἀλήθεια is contrasted with the Λήθη of line 277. Here the text mentions—among many other evils—Λήθη as a child of Eris (Discord). It is interesting to recall some lines of the gruesome catalog (*Th.* 226 ff.) in which forgetfulness finds its place in the un-

pleasant company of hardships and labors of all kinds, including Fight and
Struggle, Murder and Assassination, and intellectual flaws, including Falsehood, Discourses (Λόγους), and Disputes. Here then, Lethe (Forgetfulness)
and Falsehood are joined together in one family and are pitted against
Nereus's truthfulness and lack of Lethe (233 ff.). Concerning the etymological
play, ἀ-ληθ-, M. L. West (p. 233) writes: "Ἀληθής,-εια are often thought of
in this etymological way, and so associated with remembering, cf. *Il.* 23. 351
and many later examples collected by E. Heitsch, *Hermes*, 1962, pp. 26–30."[42]
We can add that the juxtaposition of ἀληθέα and ἀψευδέα in line 233 could even
support the idea of a conscious etymological play: ἀληθέα may be taken as a
negative term, ἀ-ληθέα and ἀ-ψευδέα thereby constituting an elegant symmetry.[43]

Nereus's truthfulness is therefore defined by his lack of forgetfulness or
neglect (235). The praise of Nereus's truthfulness follows upon a catalog of
the evil children of Eris, in which forgetfulness and falsehood are linked together. From all this evidence, we can extrapolate a set of correspondences
that reads as follows:

Truth	:	Memory	=	Falsehood	:	Forgetfulness
(Alethea)		(Mnemosyne)		(Pseudea)		(Lethe)

This set of correspondences only confirms our set of polarities: truth and
memory are opposed to falsehood and forgetfulness.[44] At this point we
might remark that the Muses' ability to call forth both memory and forgetfulness corresponds to their ability to speak a *logos* that is false, yet similar
to truth. Though an opposition between memory and oblivion is made, no
line of demarcation can be drawn between them. Exactly as in the case of
truth and falsehood, where we saw that only the Muses are capable of identification, so too, memory and oblivion are here complementary, permutable,
contiguous. In these cases the distinction is made, and the opposition shaped
and maintained, in defiance of the text. The text, we have seen, declares the
impossibility of distinguishing a false *logos* from a truthful one; does not consistently support a neat separation between straightness and crookedness; and,
finally, plays consciously on the coincidence of memory and forgetfulness.
This perplexing situation is too consistently structured to be accidental: it
must depend on a coherent principle.

One might well account for this consistent situation by assuming a special
"logic" for mythical thought. More and more classical scholars have pro-
pounded the idea that "myth" has its own particular way—often oblique, ambiguous, and unpredictable—of delivering its message.[45] Lévi-Strauss has
shown how the language of myth conveys its own logic through structures
of polarities in which permutability of terms is often the very principle of
signification. Unrestricted by an Aristotelian principle forbidding contradiction,

the mythical thought builds its meaning through polarities which are contiguous and which elicit meaningful correspondences. Speaking to similar issues, Detienne has brilliantly illustrated a whole structure of terms that define the "word" in Greek archaic thought, outlining both the oppositions and the ambiguity in the terms "truth:falsehood," etc. This ambiguity of the word represents "a particular instance of the general trait in mythical logic" (pp. 78 ff.).

The question of the "ambiguity of mythical thinking" raises some difficult problems. To begin with, in the text of Hesiod these "ambiguities" often seem to follow a textual "logic" rather than a "principle" of structural permutability *proper* to myth. For instance, if the straight discourse of the king has a deflecting power, one of the reasons is that "to persuade" in Greek implies the turning away of someone from his own line of thinking. The inevitability of the conflict between "straight" (another unaccountable metaphor) discourse and persuasion is therefore intrinsic to the Greek language. But, aside from this and analogous cases in which the paradox is rooted in the language itself, even the conceptual paradoxes elaborated by Hesiod elicit a certain logic, which provides a frame for what we call "rational" thought. There is nothing mythical in the fact that both memory and oblivion are attributes of the *logos*. The paradoxical effects of poetry have been defined and elaborated for centuries in an analogous way and in "rationalistic" terms.

The real question, then, involves precisely what is meant by mythical thinking. For, as we know, our definitions of "myth," "*logos*," and "rational" derive from that which should be defined, and they are therefore inescapably compromised. The definitions derive from the *logos* as it reveals itself in relation to *mythos* in the history of early Greek philosophy. They illustrate, in particular, the polarizing thrust of the *logos* itself, which, through the antithesis *logos*: *mythos*, reproduces for its own benefit an antinomy (and an unwanted complementarity) analogous to Hesiod's Truth:Falsehood. This does not imply that there is no difference between *mythos* and *logos* but simply that the traditional definitions are inadequate or misleading.

The impasse can be illustrated by an example. The "gift of the Muses," the central image of the paradox of the *logos*, might easily be defined as a "mythical" pattern—as the typically "mythical" representation of a complex notion. For it also involves the mythical assumption that a word of truth, fully identical to things and spoken by the gods, is a *given*—is a privilege granted to men. No rational inquiry into the nature of language, no discovery of logical patterns conducive to truth is necessary: truth is a gift, and though it has a double face, Hesiod can feel confident that the Muses have granted him the truthful *logos* since they have ritually accepted him as a devotee and a pupil.

But, as a pupil of the Muses, Hesiod learns from them the double power of their *logos*. This whole "mythical" pattern, then, elicits a "rational" discovery about the nature of language, its ambiguity, its autonomy from "things," and

therefore its power both to speak the truth and to deceive: it draws attention
to the core of the problem of language. Attempting to distinguish between
what is "rational" and what is "mythical," one finds oneself trapped in a
terrible predicament: one sees how *any* statement might be possible. Either
Hesiod's mythological pattern implies a "mythological ambiguity"—since
many gifts of the gods have parallel paradoxical qualities—or it demonstrates
the emergence of a "rational" awareness, or, finally, it constitutes a wholly
"rational" intuition set in a "mythical" shell. It is obvious that these three
statements are all possible simply because of the leeway and interplay that
our culture allows between the "mythical" and the "rational." But the question becomes more complicated when one takes into account that even the
"mythical" shell (the sheer notion of "divine gift"), is not without analogy
to themes or "figures" controlled by "rational" thought. Thus, for example,
the "gift of the Muses" can be compared with the "gift of Teuth," writing,
of which we read in the Platonic *Phaedrus*. The "logic" controlling the pharmakon there—of which Derrida has described the troubling movement[46]—
offers an instructive pattern for the paradoxical "logic" of Hesiod's *logos*.

Having advanced these general principles of caution, we might try to
identify in Hesiod's text that which is mythical and that which obeys the
logic of the Greek *logos* as defined in subsequent periods. It would appear
that the "rationalistic" kernel of Hesiod's argument rests on his distinction
between the discourse that imitates truth with difference and distortions,
and the discourse identical to truth. Since this awareness of the difference
and the effort at controlling it constitute the essential steps in subsequent
Greek "rational" thought, Hesiod's text can be judged in the light of such
later perspective. Indeed, the ways of controlling and mastering the difference will eventually move toward the formation of a "logic" alien to Hesiod.
But, for all its complexity and sophistication, such a logic will remain trapped
within the conceptual frame of imitation, and it will not escape paradoxes
and contradictions analogous, on a different level, to those of Hesiod. The
awareness that imitation implies difference from the model will force Plato
to banish poetry from his system and will ultimately lead Aristotle to insist
on the universality of mimesis, grounded on the physis, and on its value of
truth.[47]

Given the classical concept of "imitation," there is no way to elude the
difference, unless one assumes the possibility of a *perfect* re-production and
re-presentation of things, in which case imitation ceases to be. More troubling,
"imitation as difference" must be seen as the "matrix" of the oppositions of
original versus copy, truth versus falsehood. As we will demonstrate with the
example of Pandora, the original is always already a copy. This should come as no
surprise, since we have seen already that the *locus* of truth (i.e., the "original")

is always absent and manifests itself only in discourse—divine discourse, to be sure, but discourse nonetheless. We have therefore maintained that the "original" (i.e., the *locus* of truth or things as they are) is always only inscription; it is only and always contained within the *logos*. To put it another way, Hesiod's "truth" is inscribed in and circumscribed by the very literary language and tradition in which he works, and there is no way to recover this truth (the things as they are) as such.

Trapped within this logic, which is not mythical in the usual sense, Hesiod evades it by assuming the will of the Muses to tell him the real truth in the form of a discourse identical to truth. He supports this assumption with the entire literary arsenal at his disposal—the dramatization of his encounter with the Muses, the ritual of his consecration, the symbolism of honey, and so on.

As Hesiod aims at repressing the difference, the simulated identity, he sets up oppositions that correspond to the initial pair: truth versus falsehood. He coherently ranks both straightness and memory with truth, and both crookedness and oblivion with falsehood. He thus attempts to construct a metaphysical frame that should give him full control over the *logos* and its dangerous power. Interpreted in this way, the metaphysical gesture of Hesiod testifies to his confidence in the truth of his words. If, in deconstructing Hesiod's text, we have shown that the oppositions are contiguous rather than distinct, we must understand that this pattern works against the strategy of the author, the reason being that the difference which Hesiod tries to master, masters the very opposition he aims at controlling. Truth and falsehood, straightness and crookedness, etc., are therefore contiguous, not because the mythical thinker deems that a master of truth is also a master of deception, but because Hesiod cannot control the difference that marks his as any other discourse. Hesiod conceives this difference in the most general way as the discrepancy that exists in the rapport of similarity between words and things. We would, of course, give a more precise picture of that difference. Language is not only different from things because the signifier is unmotivated, but also because it constitutes a grid of differences in itself: it signifies through this structure of differences and inner references, through the lags and gaps of of spacement and temporalization. As these differences, lags, and gaps assume importance in the act of signifying, no presence can be retrieved. Yet, it is only through this difference and deferral that presence can be thought of.

INSPIRATION AND HONEY

Two crucial images control the definition of the divine essence of poetry: one presents poetry as inspiration, the breath of the Muses, the other presents it as the sweetness of honey.

Common, everyday language elicits less attention and fewer decisive insights: it, too, is a gift of the Gods (of Hephaistos in *Erga* 61 or of Hermes in *Erga* 77 ff.). The plural *Logoi* that appear as the children of Eris in *Th.* 229 may well designate the speeches of abuse and deception; some of their brothers and sisters might even be companions of the false discourse of the Muses.

Poetic language enjoys a special status: it is bestowed by the Muses only upon privileged people as a supplement to their usual language. The presentation of this special, supplementary language to Hesiod is dramatized in the encounter on Helikon with the offering of the scepter and the "breathing into" him of the divine voice (*Th.* 30 ff.). Each of these images is significant: the scepter represents the power that Hesiod receives from the Muses through their language, while the divine breathing obeys a complex logic. The breath communicates a voice almost without sound, an incorporeal whisper. Such an image accounts for both the soundless nature of inspiration and the necessity of controlling poetic language so that it adds itself to things (or the referent) without intruding with its own body and sound.

The breath of the Muses nevertheless has an imitative power. Be it false or truthful, it makes things present, visible, and audible, so that one thinks of these things as true even if they are not; but as has already been stated, only the Muses know whether they inspire with their breath a simulation of things or a genuine identity. Here we note the cautiousness of the text, for the Muses in line 28 do not claim "to sing a truth identical to true things" as the context implies and as we have suggested; rather, by announcing their divine talent with "we can sing the truth," they avoid a definition of truth in relation to the process of imitation.

The hidden logic of the breath of the Muses here becomes apparent, for since their voice is soundless and incorporeal, it adds itself to things without vicariously intruding a sound or a body of its own. Yet the image of this incorporeal breath conflicts with the other image of discourse of the Muses, sung by themselves or through the poet, which runs sweet, like honey. On the contrary, the viscosity of honey represents the thick body of words, the materiality of sound in rhythmic lines, the pleasantness of song and of music.

What, then, is the discourse of the Muses? Is it breath, animating things and uncovering them by a spiritual act that produces their simulated or real permanence? Or is it the slow ooze of a golden, viscous substance, of a sweet intoxicating liquid that induces the presence or the effacement of things?

This ambivalent description, justified even though honey and Muses' breath function on another level as parallel and analogous metaphors, embraces, in fact, the two essential views of poetry that cross the whole of our culture in perpetual conflict. In fact, the metaphor of honey paves the way for an idea of poetry as an autonomous rhetorical feat of art and technique (see Horace's *per laborem plurimum* in C. 4. 2. 29), while the metaphor of the Muses' breath, as we have seen, tends finally to repress the difference and to imply an identity between words and things as they are.

THE GIFT OF THE MUSES

Hesiod's text points to the cathartic and restorative power of the Muses' discourse that results from its almost magical quality. In fact, the discourse of the Muses, both in the mouth of the king and in that of the poet, glides over the audience smoothly, with ease and with portentous rapidity. The king's utterance restores justice *easily* ($\rho\eta\iota\delta\iota\omega\varsigma$), and that of the poet restores serenity with an instantaneous effect, *as soon as* it is heard ($\alpha\hat{\iota}\psi'$ . . . $\tau\alpha\chi\acute{\epsilon}\omega\varsigma$ [102]), as by a touch of magic.

It seems, therefore, that the inspired song of the Muses does not lose any of its magic power in passing to the human mouth of the poet. The poet always stands before his audience as if the Muses were speaking through him. He consequently finds himself in the position of divine bestower of words, as the Muses themselves are.

We should analyze the implications of this posture, especially in view of the fact that the poet seems to mimic other traits of the Muses. For one thing, the text might even suggest that the poet, singing to an audience tormented by griefs, is as free from cares as are the Muses.[48] Furthermore, he holds a rank of some sacredness, being the repository of a divine gift, a mouthpiece of the gods not unlike the prophet or seer. Consequently, the image of the Muses as bestowers of poetic song not only sustains the certitude of truth but also points to the sacredness of poetry and to its divine origin.

We shall see in the case of Pandora how the concept of the "gift" constitutes the pivot on which the "origin" of man's predicament turns. We shall then analyze the structure of the gift as an unsolicited addition to an already perfect status. In relation to poetry, however, the notion of gift, on the contrary, suggests a desirable addition, a supplementary breath granted by the gods for the temporary relief of man; furthermore, in the case of poetry, the divine gift is granted by the gods to the poet to be administered by him as their agent. It is this human administration of the divine that connotes the ideal, metaphysical portrait of the poet.

Hesiod's portrait of the poet is defined by metaphysical and elegiac traits much more than is Homer's. In the first book of the *Odyssey* we confront a text that, to a certain degree, seems to disclaim the connection between poetry and the Muses. Penelope, distressed by Phemius's narrative of the sad and inglorious return of the Greek heroes from Troy ($\nu\acute{o}\sigma\tau o\iota$), asks the poet to sing "other pleasing (or "enchanting") [themes] " ($\check{\alpha}\lambda\lambda\alpha$ $\theta\epsilon\lambda\kappa\tau\acute{\eta}\rho\iota\alpha$), namely, the "deeds of men and gods that the poets celebrate" (337-39). Though Penelope makes it clear that the poet's song is always enchanting, she cannot endure the painful theme of the heroes' return. Telemachos's answer is remarkable: he upholds the right of the poet "to please (τέρπειν) whenever his mind stirs him." He goes on to say that Zeus, not the poets, is responsible for men's sorrows. As concerns the poets, men praise them when they sing something new (345-52). The point made by Telemachos is striking, for it supports the idea of the poet's own originality, his individual responsibility, the legitimacy of his movement away from tradition. No divine inspirer is mentioned here. This creative originality—which in other passages is connected with the inspiration of the Muses (*Od*. 22. 347 ff., etc.)—is the most characteristic trait of the poet in the *Odyssey*, as Pagliaro maintains in "Aedi e rapsodi" (*Saggi di critica semantica* [Messina/Firenze, 1953], p. 11). In the debate between Penelope and Telemachos this originality is upheld, even if it leads the poet to sing a song of grief instead of a song of κλέος, as Penelope would like to hear (ἔργ᾽ ἀνδρῶν τε θεῶν τε, τά τε κλείουσιν ἀοιδοί [338], and see Nagy, pp. 225 ff.). Telemachos goes far toward justifying the song of grief: the reality of life is unescapable, and if the song of grief causes relatives of the hero to mourn, it nevertheless pleases other people; and as these others continue to celebrate (ἐπικλείουσ᾽ [351]) this song, they grant fame to the poet who sings it.

We find here some elements that will later become conventional in the portrait of the poet, but only Hesiod expands this portrait into a fully reassuring and elegiac picture. The notion of the gift, the providential ideology, and the mythical encounter with the Muses combine in outlining a unique representation: the poet appears as a divine donor, sacred and serene under the protection of the Muses, administering his magical gift to other men, spreading truth and sweetness in a world of deception and bitter contention, inducing forgetfulness into men's hearts.[49]

Each of these images has a lasting history in classical poetry: the divine donor appears in all of literature from Archilochus on, and the image of honey is a common theme from Pindar (e.g., *Ol.* 7. 7ff., frg. 152) through Theocritus (e.g., 7. 80-83) to Horace (*C.* 4. 2. 27 ff.).

Such a cluster of metaphors sustains a precise interpretation of poetry. The divine donor, whether administering his gift or the gift of the Muses, alludes to the identification of the poet as "originator" of his poetry. The poet appears in this sense as a *pater sui*, the original producer, a privileged man who possesses an original gift to distribute among others. This gift is offered generously and *gratuitously*, as the word chosen by Hesiod to represent the gift of the Muses (δῶρα [103]) seems to emphasize.[50]

In this way the production of poetry is excluded to a degree from the various modes of exchange in which it is immersed. For the poet is indebted to the poetic tradition and, more generally, to language itself; on the other hand, he sings for an audience, from whom he expects recognition (in the form of a prize). Although the concept of the Muses' inspiration may hint at the existence of a poetic tradition, Hesiod belittles his debt to it by describing his own uniquely privileged intimacy with the Muses. They often lie to their devotees, but not, presumably, to Hesiod. The awareness of this exclusiveness dictates the pungent insults that Hesiod, through the Muses, addresses to his fellow poets, both his predecessors and contemporary singers: "Shepherds of the fields, poor fools, mere bellies!" The divine donor marks here his distance from all the other poets mystified by the Muses' tricky mind.

Yet we should not be dumbfounded by the elegiac and reassuring portrait of this divine donor, freely giving his gift to a distant audience, aloof among the other poets. We know that no discourse can arise without the interference of another.[51] And Hesiod shows us unmistakably that this is the case. We know from Hesiod himself that he took part in at least one poetic competition in which he received the prize (*Erga* 654 ff.), so perhaps the gift the poet donates to his audience is not so gratuitous after all. Moreover, the violence of the insults that Hesiod addresses to his fellow poets (*Th.* 26) shows more clearly than any autobiographical event the wishfulness of his views. For these insults prove that in the act of singing, the gift of the Muses turns into a poison, in uncanny accordance with the well known semantic shift of "gift" to "poison" (Benveniste, p. 68): the oozing honey of their words turns into a sharp bite; serenity turns into hostility; aloofness turns into competition. The elegiac and reassuring portrait of the poet crumbles.

Contrary to the premises that made possible that elegiac view of poetry, the Muses' song is concerned with the others, especially with the poetic tradition and the competing poets. Furthermore, the poet's posture and stance suggest multiple modes of violence. The poet's fierce reaction to his competitors shows us that he is not aloof and, therefore, that he might also respond to the suffering of his listeners; we will even see that he himself is a victim of violence and sings like a nightingale pierced by the talons of a hawk (*Erga* 202 ff. and see chapter 3). Finally, the poet must be anxious about the truth of his song, for nothing will ever dispel the deadly implication of the Muses' statement that their lies may look just like truth (*Th.* 27).

A passage of the *Erga* (23 ff.) corroborates our view that Hesiod sings in fierce competition with his fellow poets. Hesiod equates the jealousy and resentment of other poets with that of craftsmen who compete to make the best artifact:

> . . . neighbor competes with [lit. "is envious of"
> (ζηλοῖ)] neighbor hastening to be rich. This
> Competition [Eris] is good for men. And the potter
> is resentful of the potter, the carpenter of the
> carpenter, the beggar is jealous of the beggar,
> the poet of the poet. (*Erga* 24-26).

Within this competitive context it is impossible to compare the poet's serenity
to that of his patronesses, the Muses. It is equally impossible to interpret him
as solely intent on capturing the breath of the Muses and finally becoming the
divine donor, generous and unrewarded. However, Hesiod reminds us that even
the gods demand reciprocation for their gifts; it is obviously for this reason that
he dedicates a tripod to the Muses (*Erga* 658-69). A gift always implies reciprocity and exchange.

Instead of being solely intent on the Muses' inspiration, instead of repeating the secret ceremony of the Helikon each time he composes, Hesiod glances
at his competitors with jealousy. In fact, it is Eris who compels the competi-
tor to look at his neighbor:

> For one who needs work, *seeing* (ἰδών) another man
> who is rich, hastens to plow and to plant and to set
> his house in order,[52] and neighbor competes with neighbor. . . .
> (*Erga* 21 ff.)

This glance to the side, this gazing with excitement at his fellow poets, is fatal
for the straight discourse of Hesiod, for only the man who works and speaks
intent on himself alone (if this is possible) can move straight ahead, in a direct
line. Hesiod makes the point when, in the *Erga*, he speaks of the good laborer.
A good laborer, he says, can plow furrows in perfectly straight lines, but a
young man cannot perform the same task as well. The inability of the young
man does not result from inexperience, but rather, Hesiod continues, from
the distraction of gazing "with excitement at his fellow laborers" (μεθ'
ὁμήλικας ἐπτοίηται [*Erga* 447]). Mazon defines this last line as a "*boutade*."
But the crookedness of the line, of the *logos*, or of the dikê must be represented by the same conceptual image; and, in fact, in all these cases the
deviation takes place due to an intrusion of an otherness into the self.

We have reached a crucial point: here again the lines of our inquiry con-
verge in undoing the Hesiodean fabric and in suggesting an emphasis on the
terms discarded by Hesiod. The *logos* deviates not only because it persuades
but also because the eyes of the poet and his excited attention are turned
toward fellow poets. The Muses, witnesses to "things as they are," sole
link between the poet and truth, are on a different trajectory: the poet
looks at them only askance. Thus, in reality, the poetic *logos*, like the poet's
vision, moves neither in a straight nor in a crooked line, but askew; straightness and crookedness are the metaphysical terms of an opposition that the
poet relies on to sustain his fabric, but the discourse outlines an oblique
movement, through a vacillating rhythm—a constant detour and displacement. The desire to stride straight to "things as they are" and to mirror them
marks the text with neat polarizations, but underneath these polarizations

the *logos* undoes that fabric. The fabric and its undoing coexist in a powerful and unresolved tension.

In addition, the idea of competition demonstrates that the conception of the poet as donor must accommodate a process of exchange between the poet and the poetic tradition, between him and his fellow poets, between him and his audience; an element of "market economy" is thereby superimposed onto the image of divine donation.

Such an exchange, in its deepest significance, implies the relationship between Hesiod's text and the texture of the language in which he sings.[53] Several questions arise with regard to this relationship, specifically that of the authorial voice—that is, of the mark left by Hesiod upon the culture and poetic tradition in which he worked. There is no doubt that the poet was conscious of his own originality and of the particular "signature" that he imprinted on his text. He was the first Greek poet we know who put his own name on the text of a poem.

αἵ νύ ποθ᾽ Ἡσίοδον καλὴν ἐδίδαξαν ἀοιδήν
(*Th.* 22)

[The Muses] who taught Hesiod a beautiful song

The verse, as far as we know, has only a slight formulaic trace;[54] on the contrary, it strikes one as unconventional and original because of the mention of the name of the poet and because of the probable pun on the words Ἡσίοδον (etymologically, "sender forth of song") and ἀοιδήν ("song").[55]

For all Hesiod's pride in this exhibition of his name, the signature does not entirely *appropriate* the song of the Muses. For the Muses failed to teach their pupil, Hesiod, the impossible secret that would have empowered him to ascertain the truth of their song. Falling short of this, the poet still sings *their* song. This means that Hesiod's language, for all its originality, is still the language of others: his diction is heavily epic and is indebted to a historical tradition; his myths and his culture derive from a long past. Hesiod's own poetic *logos* entertains a relationship of difference with its linguistic and cultural tradition, as will be shown in the course of the study.

Likewise, the gift cannot be a "unicum" given once and for all, a mirror and expansion of what is the self's "own." The gift is ruled by the economic process of exchange, and this same process teaches us again the "fiction" of that which is "own" and "proper."[56]

The material and evidence concerning Hesiod's views on truth and falsehood have been collected and analyzed extensively. In recent years various works have appeared:

Detienne, M. *Les maîtres de vérité dans la Grèce archaïque.* Paris, 1967.
(Hereafter cited as Detienne.)

Lain Entralgo, P. *The Therapy of the Word in Classical Antiquity.* New Haven, 1970.

Lanata, G. *Poetica pre-platonica, testimonianze e frammenti.* Florence, 1963.

Luther, W. "Wahrheit, Licht und Erkenntniss in der Griechischen Philosophie bis Democrit." *Archiv für Begriffsgeschichte* 10 (1966): 1-240. (Hereafter cited as Luther.)

—"*Wahrheit*" *und* "*Lüge*" *in ältesten Griechentum.* Leipzig, 1935.

My analysis is somewhat parallel to that of M. Detienne, but our classifications of evidence and interpretations are different. M. Detienne is particularly concerned with the mythical and sociological structure that frames and provides connotations for these various notions. My analysis tries to show the structure that these notions form in the text.

An earlier and shorter version of this chapter has appeared in *Poetry and Poetics from Ancient Greece to the Renaissance: Studies in Honor of James Hutton*, ed. G. M. Kirkwood. (Ithaca, N.Y.: Cornell University Press, 1975.)

NOTES

1.   Hesiod refers to the poetic song in various ways: ἀοιδή (*Th.* 22, etc.), ὑμνεῖν (*Th.* 34, etc.); but also λέγειν (*Th.* 27) and *logos* (*Erga* 106). See p. 5.

2.   ἄλλοτε δ' ἀλλοῖος Ζηνὸς νόος αἰγιόχοιο,
ἀργαλέος δ' ἄνδρεσσι καταθνητοῖσι νοῆσαι.

"Sometimes Zeus is of one mind, sometimes of another mind,

and it is difficult for mortal man to understand."

Ἄλλοτε δ' ἀλλοῖος is *hapax* in Hesiod, and the expression is unprecedented. For Zeus's capacity for deception, see *Th.* 889-90 and Detienne, pp. 64 ff.

3.   Hom. *Il.* 18. 328, Aesch. *Supp.* 86, etc.

4.   For Hesiod to describe the mind of Zeus (*Erga* 658-62) according to the teaching of the Muses implies a song that, because of its immensity, not even a god could sing (ἀθέσφατος ὕμνος [*Erga* 662]). For this meaning of the epithet see Apoll. Soph., quoted by U. von Wilamowitz-Möllendorff in *Hesiodos Erga,* 3d. ed. (Dublin/Zürich, 1970) p. 117. On the other hand, see the interpretations of H. Fränkel, *Antidoron: Festschrift J. Wackernagel* (Göttingen, 1923), pp. 281-82, who translates the epithet as "as it pleases, i.e., whatever the Muses and the poet want to sing" and of E. Benveniste, *Indo-European Language and Society* (Miami, 1971), pp. 414 ff., who inter-

prets the epithet as "boundless": Hesiod's song would then know no limits. Finally, Chantraine, *Dictionnaire étymologique de la langue Grecque*, (Paris, 1967), presents the alluring hypothesis that ἀθέσφατος may be a simple doublet of θέσφατος "announced, determined by the gods," the initial a- being possibly pleonastic and not privative.

5.　Line 27 repeats *Od.* 19. 203 with small variations: ἴσκε ψεύδεα πολλὰ λέγων ἐτύμοισιν ὁμοῖα. M. L. West finds Hesiod's ἴδμεν . . . λέγειν to be a happier expression than the Homeric one. In fact, ἴσκε must be a present of ἔοικα, in the factitive sense of "making similar," and it therefore repeats the notion of ὁμοῖα. On the question of the priority of Hesiod's or Homer's text, see F. Solmsen, "The 'Gift' of Speech in Homer and Hesiod," *TAPA* 85 (1954): 11 ff.; G. P. Edwards, *The Language of Hesiod in Its Traditional Context*, (Oxford, 1971), pp. 16 ff.

6.　As concerns the formulaic style of the text itself, *Th.* 26 shows the combination of two formulae that we know from Homer (*Il.* 18. 162; 5. 787; 8. 228); *Th.* 27 forms a unique parallel with *Od.* 19. 203. In fact, both ψεύδεα πολλὰ and πολλὰ . . . λέγειν constitute verbal connections that are unique in these two passages; the position of ψεύδεα in the second place of the line is again unique, since of the five other instances of ψεύδεα in Homer and Hesiod, the word occupies the initial position four times (*Od.* 11. 366; 14. 296; *Erga* 78 and 789) and (*Th.* 229) occurs between the second and the third foot once (ψεύδεᾱ synizesis). *Th.* 28 appears to contain elements of innovation: as Edwards has noticed (p. 53), ἀληθέα γηρύσασθαι stand beside ἀληθέα μυθήσασθαι of *Il.* 6. 382; *Od.* 14. 125; 17. 15; 18. 342.

7.　Ὁμοῖος, "similar," "same," "equal," from ὁμός connected with a large Indo-European group of words: Persian *hama*, "similar," "same"; Gothic *sama* "similar," "same," etc. See H. Frisk, *Griechisches etymologisches Wörterbuch* 2 vols. (Heidelberg, 1960), s.v. ὁμός.

In Hesiod the word indicates "similarity," as between father and sons (*Erga* 182), or "sameness" (*Erga* 114). Luther, p. 100, n. 131, maintains that in the early Greek mind, the concept ὁμοῖος does not distinguish between "similarity" and "equality."

8.　Luther, pp. 30 ff., maintains that the archaic Greek language and mind do not distinguish between "real" (*wirklich*) and "truthful" (*wahr*). Thus, for instance, the "real," "actual" return of Odysseus is ἐτήτυμος νόστος (*Od.* 3. 241) exactly as the truthful words of Eurycleia are μῦθος ἐτήτυμος (*Od.* 23. 62 ff.).

9.　Ἔτυμος means something which has truly happened (see Tilman Krischer, "ΕΤΥΜΟΣ und ΑΛΗΘΗΣ," *Philologus* 109 [1965]: 166-67). See also H. Hommel, "Wahrheit und Gerechtigkeit. Zur Geschichte und Deutung eines Begriffspaars," *Antike und Abendland* 15 (1969): 174: "Daneben stehet in

älterer Zeit das ἐτεόν auch ἔτυμον oder ἐτήτυμον das 'Seinsmässige, Echte, Wirch-
liche.' " See also Hjalmar Frisk, "Wahrheit und Lüge in d. Indog. Sprachen" in
Kleine Schriften zur Indogermanistik und zur griechischen Wortkunde (Stock-
holm, 1966), pp. 3 ff., and in particular his conclusion on the word ἐτεός and
cognates:

> Freilich lässt sich schwerlich sagen, welche Anschauung mit dem
> uralten, sicher urindogermanischen Begriff, der in *satyá-*, ἐτεός,
> *sons, sannr, istū* usw. reflektiert wird, ursprünglich verknüpft war.
> Das Verbum **es* hat schon in der Ursprache die Bedeutung 'es gibt,
> ist vorhanden' angenommen, und mithin können wir auch für dessen
> nominale Formen hinter die allgemeine Bedeutung 'befindlich, tat-
> sächlich existierend' nicht dringen.
>
> (p. 31)

'Αληθής instead is the account of something that the speaker himself has ex-
perienced, an account that does not leave anything unnoticed. See Krischer,
"ΕΤΥΜΟΣ," pp. 163 and 167.

On the etymology of ψεῦδος we do not have anything certain. See Frisk,
"Wahrheit" pp. 16 ff., and the treatment of the word in his *Griechisches
etymologiches Wörterbuch.*

For the opposition ἔτυμα : ψεῦδος see, in addition to *Od.* 19. 203, *Il.* 10.
538 and *Od.* 4. 140.

10.   I should make clear that in *Od.* 4. 348 there is explicit reference to deception, not to falsehood; but the idea of falsehood is implicit: see *Od.* 4.
331.

11.   The statement of the Muses has been sometimes taken *only* to mean
that Homeric epic is false, though it is inspired by the Muses (see Luther,
pp. 41 ff.). This interpretation is true, but restrictive: it fails to explain the
whole sentence of the Muses. They do *not* simply say: "We know how to say
false things, though if we want, we can sing true ones." The Muses make a
more intriguing assertion: "We know how to say false things that look like
true ones." I question this expression, and I recognize here a "paradox": the
sense that language *imitates* true things yet remains different from them. I
reject, therefore, the banal interpretation that would take all these terms
(imitation, ἀλήθεια, etc.), as unproblematic terms.

12.   K. Latte ("Das Rechtsgedanke im archaischen Griechentum," *Antike
und Abendland* 2 [1946] :160) maintains that the meaning of ἐτήτυμα in *Erga*
10 is "the content of a representation or of a statement congruent to the
actual [real, *wirklich*] facts [*Sachverhalt*] ." Luther (see n. 8) maintains that
the archaic mind does not distinguish between *"wirklich"* and *"wahr."* The
question is complicated by the fact that the *logos* itself, for the Greeks, is
not a "form" or a "tool," but a real *being*. See Luther, p. 32.

13.   Aristotle's definition of language as a conventional symbol (σύμβολα) of conceptual impressions (παθήματα τῆς ψυχῆς [Int. 16a 5 ff.]) parallels that of language as symbol (σύμβολα) of things (Soph. El. 1. 165a 7): τοῖς ὀνόμασιν ἀντὶ τῶν πραγμάτων χρώμεθα συμβόλοις.

14.   For an illuminating discussion of these and other passages, see E. Norden, P. Vergilius Maro, Aeneis Buch VI 4th ed. (Darmstadt, 1957), p. 208, and the brilliant analysis by G. Nagy, Comparative Studies in Greek and Indic Meter, (Cambridge, Mass. 1976) pp. 244 ff., and especially pp. 248 ff. I translate here two of the most significant Greek passages. In Il. 2. 484 ff. the poet invokes the Muses before starting the long catalog of the ships:

> "Tell me, Muses who dwell in the palaces of Olympus,
> for you are goddesses and you are present (πάρεστε)
> and know all things, but we [the poets] hear only a
> rumor (κλέος) and do not know anything. . . ."

The second is Gorgias Hel. 2: ". . . about whom [Helen], the confidence [or "testimony," πίστις] of the inspired poets [lit., "of the poets who have heard," namely, the κλέος] has become concord and unanimous. . . ."

Hes. Th. 30–34 diverges from the above examples, in the extent to which Hesiod emphasizes his encounter with the Muses themselves. Yet here, too, they "inspire" (Th. 31 ff. [or, as in Erga 662, "teach"]) the poet; and, in fact, the song they inspire is a κλέος about the past and the future (ἵνα κλείοιμι [32]). Hesiod, therefore, renews the theme—at least for us—by narrating his encounter with the Muses: he sees them and he is ritually empowered to repeat their song. This enhances his confidence in the good intention of the Muses and in their willingness to tell him the truth.

15.   The whole of archaic and classical Greek thought makes "the things" (τὰ ὄντα) the locus of truth and the logos the possible way to truth.

16.   For the problems hinted at here, see my Euripides' Tragic Discourse and the Medea (Ithaca, New York: forthcoming).

17.   See A. Momigliano, "Prodico di Ceo e le dottrine sul linguaggio da Democrito ai cinici," Atti R. Accademia delle Scienze di Torino 65 (1929–30): 95-107. Not all sophists hold the same view: I am thinking here especially of Gorgias, Protagoras, and the influential figure of Democritus.

In his treatise On Not Being or On Nature, Gorgias writes, "that which we communicate is the logos, but the logos is not substance and existing things (τὰ ὑποκείμενα καὶ ὄντα). We therefore do not communicate to others existing things but rather the logos which is different (ἕτερος) from these things." On Gorgias, see C. P. Segal, "Gorgias and the Psychology of the Logos," HSCP 66 (1962): 99-155.

18.   J. Derrida, "La pharmacie de Platon," in Dissemination (Paris, 1972).

19.   For Aristotle see P. Aubenque, *Le Problème de l'être chez Aristote* (Paris, 1962) and J. Derrida, "La mythologie blanche" in *Marges* (Paris, 1972). For the problem in Western thought, see J. Derrida, *De la grammatologie*, (Paris, 1967).

One can hardly refrain from quoting from a famous passage of Nietzsche, who was one of the first modern philosophers to recognize the connection between language and all metaphysics and therefore to understand the goal of philosophy as a new scrutiny of language:

> Was ist also Wahrheit? Ein bewegliches Heer von Metaphern, Metonymien, Anthropomorphismen, kurz eine Summe von menschlichen Relationen, die, poetisch und rhetorisch gesteigert, übertragen, geschmückt wurden, und die nach langem Gebrauch einem Volke fest, kanonisch und verbindlich dünken: die Wahrheiten sind Illusionen, von denen man vergessen hat, dass sie welche sind, Metaphern, die abgenutzt und sinnlich kraftlos geworden sind, Münzen, die ihr Bild verloren haben und nun als Metall, nicht mehr als Münzen, in Betracht kommen.

Das Philosophenbuch 3. Kröner 10, 195.

20.   Some of Derrida's works have already been translated into English: see *Speech and Phenomena, and Other Essays on Husserl's Theory of Signs*, trans. David B. Allison (Evanston, 1973); *Of Grammatology*, trans. Gayatri Chakravorty Spivak (Baltimore: Johns Hopkins University Press, 1976).

21.   "Ἀσφαλέος, unerringly. The idea of truth is often associated with that of ἀσφάλεια" (West, p. 184; he quotes various passages from Pindar on). The steadfastness of this *logos* is remarkable, because elsewhere in the *Theogony*, *Erga*, and *Aspis* only Earth and Uranos deserve that epithet (*Th.* 117 and 128).

22.   Solmsen ("The 'Gift' of Speech," p. 6) writes that "truth" and "straight" sentences do not seem to lie on the same plane for Hesiod. But in note 18 Solmsen adds, "I am not altogether sure of this; note that at *Theog.* 233 Nereus is extolled as ἀληθής (ἀψευδής, νημερτής) as well as δίκαιος (235 ff.) He is also called ἤπιος, which word in turn is very close to μείλιχος (see the use of both words in the verses on Leto, 407 ff.)." On the passage *Th.* 233 see below, pp. 23–24. On the relationship between ἀλήθεια and δίκη in the mythical thought, see Detienne, chap. 3.

23.   On Hesiod's novelty in defining eloquent speech as a precise gift of the Muses, see Solmsen, "The 'Gift' of Speech," p. 5: "Effective speech is for Hesiod not one of the two outstanding excellences of man but one of the two gifts of the Muses. Where the poets of the *Iliad* and *Odyssey* say "Zeus" or "a god," or "The gods have given" and leave it at that without wishing to scrutinize things any further, Hesiod finds himself able to identify the giver precisely." Solmsen also notes that "this seems to be the only instance in which Hesiod expanded the sphere of a deity whom he knew from tradition."

24. This seems a possible interpretation of the Greek. See West for other interpretations.

25. LSJ translates μετάτροπα ἔργα more literally, with "deeds that turn upon their author."

26. Ἀγορῆφι is here taken with βλαπτομένοις "in their dealings" (West).

27. Solmsen, "The 'Gift' of Speech," p. 7: "The Kings whom Hesiod here has in mind do not *impose* judgments but rely on their gift of gentle persuasion—an appeal to reason—to settle the disputes. Hesiod draws his picture of the kings who give straight verdicts and do so by persuasion in opposition to the *Iliad* passage from which he borrows the phrase (δια) κρίνειν θέμιστας (*Il.* 16. 387 ff.)."

28. On the meaning of the preverb παρά-, cf. E. Schwyzer, *Griechische Grammatik* 2 vols. (Munich, 1939), 2: 493: "vorbei und zu etwas anderem übergehen, eine Veränderung bewirken: π.πείθω, -πλάσσω, -φημι, ..."

Though the active use of the verb παράφημι seems little affected by the preposition παρά- (see *Il.* 1. 577, where Hephaistos "advises" his mother), the use of the middle shows, in Homer, the notion of "misleading," or "passing over." See *Il.* 12. 248 f:

ἠέ τιν' ἄλλον
παρφάμενος ἐπέεσσιν ἀποστρέψεις πολέμοιο

Here the idea of "persuading someone" parallels in this context that of "leading someone astray," as it is emphasized by ἀποστρέψεις.

ἔνθ' ἔνι μὲν φιλότης ἐν δ' ἵμερος ἐν δ' ὀαριστὺς
πάρφασις, ἥ τ' ἔκλεψε νόον πύκα περ φρονεόντων
(*Il.* 14. 216, 217)

Πάρφασις is one of the ingredients of Aphrodite's κέστος: it deceives (ἔκλεψε) the mind (Detienne, pp. 67 ff.). In *Od.* 2. 189 we read of an old man who persuades or misleads a young one and excites him until he becomes troublesome: παρφάμενος ἐπέεσσιν ἐποτρύνῃς χαλεπαίνειν. In *Od.* 16. 287; 19. 6 the same verb with μαλακοῖσ' ἐπέεσσιν means "to calm down, to reassure" and implies deception. See also *Od.* 18. 178, where παραυδάω may have a similar connotation of deception and deviousness. For the meaning of "deceive" after Hesiod, see West's commentary.

29. See West *ad loc.*: "παρά- has the same force as in παραιφάμενος, παραμυθεῖσθαι." On both passages, 90 ff. and 103, see H. Fränkel, *Dichtung und Philosophie des frühen Griechentums* (New York, 1951), p. 150, who observes the parallelism of expression for "das Tun des Königs und des Sängers." Notice that παρατρέπειν λόγον (Hdt. 3. 2) means to falsify a story. See also Detienne, p. 73, n. 133, on the rhetorical fortune of the word.

30. Since we are in a speculative realm, let us also notice the oddity of the name "Helikon," the mountain where the Muses meet Hesiod. The toponym "Helikon" (Ἑλικών) has often been connected by etymologists with *Vimi-*

nalis and interpreted as "the mountain of willows" (Fick, Solmsen; and see also P. Chantraine, *Dict. étym.,* s.v. Ἑλικών, but the more recent philologists, such as H. Frisk (*Griechisches etymologisches Wörterbuch,* s.v. Ἑλικών) and Chantraine, feel that if the word is Greek, the proposed etymology, while possible, is far from proved. On the one hand, "the mountain of willows" would be applied correctly only to well-watered valleys; on the other hand, it would imply a word for the willow other than *ἑλικᾶ,* i.e., Ϝελικᾶ (Chantraine). Whatever the etymology may be, the connection between the word "Helikon" and ἕλιξ can scarcely be avoided: the general idea of winding or of a spiral is certainly evoked by the toponym. This suggestion, however, is not made explicit in the text through the use of puns or other stylistic devices.

31.   The sweetness of speech is a common quality, one which we find in the song of the poet, in the eloquence of the righteous king (*Th.* 83-84), and in the truthfulness of the righteous Nereus (*Th.* 235-36: νημερτής τε καὶ ἤπιος . . . καὶ ἤπια δήνεα οἶδεν.) See Solmsen, "The 'Gift' of Speech," p. 6, n. 18, and Detienne, p. 40.

32.   The verb μειλίσσω implies distortion of truth in *Od.* 3. 96, etc.

33.   On the symbolism of honey see W. Robert Tornow, *De apium mellisque significatione symbolica et mythologica* (Berlin, 1893). We should perhaps call attention to the verb ῥεῖ that defines the flowing of honey: later poetry will often be described as a running stream.

34.   The poet of the *Iliad* is less fascinated by the skill of the honey-speaking persuader. The ironic portrait of Nestor in *Il.* 1. 247 ff. even suggests a mild devaluation of this rhetoric. The old man is defined in an accumulated series of "sweet" epithets: "sweetly speaking" (ἡδυεπής), "clear speaking" (λιγύς— an epithet not infrequently used for the Muses), and possessing a voice that "runs from his tongue sweeter than honey." The hyperbole seems to make fun of the simile in its positive form.

35.   On these mysterious sisters see the commentary by T. W. Allen, W. R. Halliday, and E. E. Sikes on the *Homeric Hymns* (Oxford, 1936), p. 346; E. Benveniste, *Indo-European Language and Society,* p. 332; and F. Càssola, *Inni omerici* (Milan, 1975), pp. 543 ff.

On honey as a source of inspiration see the passages quoted in the commentary: Pind. *Pyth.* 4. 60, *Il.* 6. 47, Ar. *Ranae* 1274, etc.

36.   In particular we may recall Nestor's proposal to soothe Achilles' wrath by means of "pleasing gifts and honey-like words" (*Il.* 9. 111-113), or the passage in *Od.* 1. 56-57 where Calypso "enchants" Odysseus "with soft and wily words" (μαλακοῖσι καὶ αἱμυλίοισι λόγοισι θέλγει) "so that he may *forget* Ithaca" (ὅπως Ἰθάκης ἐπιλήσεται).

37.   See Tornow, *De apium,* p. 128 ff.

38.   West calls this juxtaposition "a conscious paradox."

39.   The formula of line 32 could indeed be equivalent, as West maintains, to the formula of line 38. But the variation on the formula should nonetheless be remarked on, especially in view of the fact that the song of the poet turns away the "present grief" (*Th.* 98 ff.), and sings the κλέος of men of old and of the gods.

40.   Detienne, pp. 29-50.

41.   We should not press this point too much, for the *forgetfulness* of crooked, unjust decisions (*Erga* 264) would identify forgetfulness with truth and straightness. But, like Nereus, Zeus is characterized by lack of λήθη:

> καί νυ τάδ᾿, αἴ κ᾿ ἐθέλῃ, ἐπιδέρκεται, οὐδέ ἑ λήθει,
> οἵην δὴ καὶ τήνδε δίκην πόλις ἐντὸς ἐέργει.
>
> (*Erga* 268-69)

Here λήθει has the normal active meaning: "escape notice."

42.   "La notion mythique d᾿ ΑΛΗΘΕΙΑ, an important paper by M. Detienne on the relationship between Ἀλήθεια and λήθη, appeared in *REG* 73 (1960): 27 ff. See also his book *Les maîtres de vérité*, pp. 9-27, 105 ff.

See Tilman Krischer, "ΕΤΥΜΟΣ und ΑΛΗΘΗΣ," pp. 161-74 and in particular p. 165, n. 1, where he connects ἀληθής of *Th.* 233 with Λήθη of *Th.* 227.

We should make clear that today the accepted etymology of ἀλήθεια mainly derives from the active meaning of λανθάνω, " to pass unnoticed, unperceived," though the connection of ἀλήθεια with λανθάνομαι ("forgetfulness," "to forget") is supported by scholars (see Luther, pp. 35 ff.), and in fact it has been emphasized by the Greek texts since *Il.* 23. 361. Luther, p. 36, reconciles both etymological connections.

On the matter of being true as "being uncovered" and "uncoveredness," see Heidegger, *Being and Time*, (New York, 1962), pp. 262 ff.

43.   The Greek taste for the alliterated repetition of negative words is well known: in Hesiod see *Th.* 277, 489, 797, 944.

Notice that P. Friedlander, Plato 1.² 1954, p. 235 denies that the Greeks felt the etymological origin of ἀλήθεια in their spoken language. M. Detienne, "La notion mythique d᾿ ΑΛΗΘΕΙΑ," p. 33, states that the relationship between the two religious representations πεδίον Λήθης and πεδίον Ἀληθείας "nous restitue un plan de la conscience où l᾿ α- privatif avait sa pleine valeur, et c᾿est un plan mythique." H. D. Rankin, "ΑΛΗΘΕΙΑ in Plato," *Glotta* 41 (1963): 51 ff., infers Plato's awareness of the negative force of ἀλήθεια from Plato's usage of the same two expressions. Luther, p. 33, argues from *Od.* 13. 254 ff. that the living language did in fact feel the negative force of ἀλήθεια.

44.   One slowly becomes aware that the polarity "memory:forgetfulness" also implies the polarity "self:other." The memory of the Muses—the song of the other—effaces the self. And this is true in a double sense: the poet forgetful of himself is simply repeating the song that the Muses have taught him, and his listeners forget themselves. But as the Muses constitute the hypostatization of Hesiod's self, the polarity is turned into a self that aims at possessing others and at making them forgetful of themselves.

45.   See, for instance, H. Fränkel, *Dichtung und Philosophie*, and B. A. van Groningen, *La composition littéraire archaïque grecque* (Amsterdam, 1958).

46.   Derrida, "La pharmacie de Platon."

47.   See Derrida, "La mythologie blanche."

48.   The Muses are pointedly described as totally free of concerns in their own hearts and involved with their singing:

$$\tilde{\eta}\sigma\iota\nu\ \dot{\alpha}o\iota\delta\dot{\eta}$$
$$\mu\acute{\epsilon}\mu\beta\lambda\epsilon\tau\alpha\iota\ \dot{\epsilon}\nu\ \sigma\tau\acute{\eta}\theta\epsilon\sigma\sigma\iota\nu,\ \dot{\alpha}\kappa\eta\delta\acute{\epsilon}\alpha\ \theta\upsilon\mu\grave{o}\nu\ \dot{\epsilon}\chi o\acute{\upsilon}\sigma\alpha\iota\varsigma,$$
$$(Th.\ 60\text{–}61)$$

(The expression ἀκηδέα θυμὸν ἐχούσαις is Hesiodic, i.e., un-Homeric. See West, p. 176.) The Muses, "inside themselves," feel concerned only with song: they are free from cares or griefs. The situation of the poet should be similar, though the text does not enlighten us on this point. This omission has no bearing on our argument; but, in view of the facts that the poet is the Muses' pupil and that the theme of their song is the same (i.e., "the true-hearted manners of the immortals"[*Th.* 66]), we might assume that the Muses' care-free attitude and exclusive concern for their song constitute the poet's ideal condition. Thus, at least ideally, the poetic song flows from a heart free of care; but in its path it confronts men's griefs. The expression ἀκηδέα θυμόν, applied to the Muses (61), is explicitly posited against the locution πένθος ἔχων νεοκηδεί θυμῷ (98), applied to the men for whom the poet sings.

49.   The *logos* of the Muses is healing, since it effaces the anguish and the pain of men. In the elaborate structure of Hesiodic oppositions, the sweetness and healing power of the word are connected with its truth and memory. The oblivious discourse, inducing forgetfulness, is, on the contrary, connected with violence and death. The *logos* of Lethe is a son of Eris and therefore a brother of Hunger and Anguish, of Struggle, Battle, Murder, Homicide and Quarrels, of Lie and Dispute (*Th.* 226 ff.). But since the whole structure of oppositions has revealed itself to be a structure of contiguous terms, we can safely say that the healing virtue of the word is akin to its violence and its power of forgetfulness and death.

50.   See E. Benveniste, *Indo-European Language and Society*, pp. 54 ff.

51.   For Aristotle as well, the fundamental condition of human discourse lies in the fact that it is always a discourse for the other: "For it is a universal

habit for the inquirers to aim not at the object itself but at the contradictor; and even when one inquires by himself he advances until he is no longer able to contradict himself" (Arist. *De Caelo* 294b.) See Aubenque, *Le problème de l'être chez Aristote*, p. 114.

52.   Lines 21-23 are difficult because of textual uncertainties, and various texts offer the possibility of various interpretations; see n. 7 of the conclusions.

53.   On the transient status of formulaic diction in Hesiod, see A. Hoekstra, *Homeric Modifications of Formulaic Prototypes*, (Amsterdam/London, 1969), pp. 83 ff., and Edwards, *The Language of Hesiod*.

54.   While the position of ἀοιδή in the line is formulaic for both Homer and Hesiod, neither the epithet καλήν nor the verbal connection with διδάσκω occurs elsewhere. In *Erga* 662 Hesiod connects διδάσκω with ὕμνον ἀείδειν, and in *Od.* 8. 479-80, the poet connects διδάσκω with οἴμαι, i.e., the themes of the song or the "trace" of it as Pagliaro understands the word (p. 34 ff.).

55.   See West, p. 161.

56.   Through the exchange, the circumscription and the role of that which is "owned" by the self and the other are fictionally established. As R. Gasché has recently written:

> "Tout échange ne devient possible . . . que par le projet
> de récupération par un moi, d'un propre aliéné, moi qui
> toutefois se conçoit hors du cercle et par là-même comme
> une plénitude irréductible, leurre autant que l'objet
> jeté dans le circuit, qui n'est que le substitut de son
> propre. Cet échange premier de ce qui aurait été perdu,
> ouvre et limite l'échange. Cette aliénation du propre
> est fictive, puisque le moi qui entre dans l'échange se
> croit extérieur par rapport à lui, se croit plénitude
> irréductible par l'occultation de l'aliénation originaire,
> qui fait qu'il est toujours déjà pris dans l'échange et
> qui s'ajoute à celle-ci comme une répétition de cette perte
> originaire, répétition qui procure l'illusion d'une perte
> conditionnelle récupérable. Et comme . . . cet échange
> ne se pratique que pour le prestige et pour l'acquisition de
> "surplus," nous pouvons en déduire que cet échange et
> l'aliénation fictive qui l'ouvre, est essentiellement la
> logique de la production de la propriété. Le fantasme du
> propre en serait la condition. (*L'Arc* 48 (1972): 80-81).

This passage clearly illustrates the fiction of that which is "own" and "proper." In the process of exchange the self and the other alternately assume an outside position in which "that which is owned" plays a momentary and fictional role as if it were fully "own," present, and controlled. By this position and role the self gains mastery over the other, only to find itself in the reverse position at the next exchange. Through this oscillation of roles, the process of exchange repeats, as it were, the assumption that an "original" unique gift exists. In reality such a repetition unveils the absence of any original gift, in a manner not unlike that whereby the imitation and repetition of language only repeat the absence of an "original" model. The process of exchange therefore at once hides and exposes the "original" indebtedness of that which is wanted and illustrates the *supplementary* movement of its repetition.

Bearing these findings in mind, we can assess the complexity of Hesiod's stance. Here again we find that Hesiod superimposes a "mythical" view of the role of the poet onto a "rationalistic" one. In the "mythical" representation, we see the poet standing aloof, outside the world of his addresses, administering a gift—a unicum—that makes him master charmer of men. This representation elicits a metaphysics of the presence, of that which is fully and irreducibly "own." On the other hand, in the "rationalistic" representation, we see the poet, in competition with his fellow poets, exchanging his gift for a prize. This process reveals the movement of supplementarity of the gift-exchange, leaving the metaphysics of presence concealed and covered. By deconstructing with Gasché the strategy of this process (of the *logos*), we realize that the same metaphysics of presence underlies the "rationalistic" view as well. *Logos* and *mythos* are therefore trapped within the same metaphysics. However, whereas the "myth" declares its metaphysical preoccupation directly, the *logos* hides it, and only through a detour that declares the supplementarity of the process, aims at recovering the same presence.

Chapter 2
DIKÊ AND LOGOS

Justice will overtake the fabricators of lies
and false witnesses.

Heraclitus, frg. 28 (D.K.)

THE STRAIGHT DIKÊ

Recent discussions of the etymological origins of dikê have not paid sufficient attention to the connections between dikê and *logos* and the polarity straight:crooked. With a view to the etymology of dikê, scholars have tended to trace this polarity back to an "original" sense of dikê. Before confronting this problem we should first survey the evidence provided by the texts.

From the beginning of the *Erga*,[1] Hesiod establishes a connection between this polarity, straight:crooked, and the concept of justice (dikê). Zeus, the god who straightens crookedness (*Erga* 7), is begged to straighten legal decisions or laws according to justice: δίκη δ᾽ ἴθυνε θέμιστας (*Erga* 9).[2] In this passage, dikê is defined as a straight line or as an abstract notion of right that is able to impose straightness. Dikê is also found in the plural, and it means either the "right" or "crooked" verdicts or decisions (e.g., *Erga* 215-30, 262). The violation of justice is expressed by a metaphor that implies—as does the English "transgression"—deviation from a straight line.

Hesiod describes kings (*basileis*) who render unjust verdicts as men who *deflect* (straight) *judgments by means of crooked words* (*Erga* 262): ἄλλῃ παρκλίνωσι δίκας σκολιῶς ἐνέποντες. The parallelism between "deflecting the rights or the verdicts" and "speaking crookedly" is obvious. The verb παρακλίνω

45

is analogous in formation to παράφημι and παρατρέπω (*Th.* 90 and 103) which, as we saw, describe the "deviation" the king's *logos* causes in others' minds and the diversion created by the song of the Muses.

In the *Odyssey* (4. 348) the adverb παρακλιδόν is used for speaking "oblique-ly."[3] In another Hesiodic passage, transgressors of justice (δίκαιον) are defined by the verb παρεκβαίνειν, "to deviate from":

> οἳ δὲ δίκας ξείνοισι καὶ ἐνδήμοισι διδοῦσιν
> ἰθείας καὶ μή τι παρεκβαίνουσι δικαίου,
> (*Erga* 225-26)

> [those] who give straight verdicts to foreigners and citizens
> and do not transgress justice. . .

The verb παρεκβαίνειν in this metaphorical meaning is parallel to παραβαίνω (παραιβασία [*Th.* 220]), ὑπερβαίνω (ὑπερβασία [*Il.* 3. 206]) and παρακλίνω (παρακλιδόν [see n. 3]), all meaning "deviation from" or "deflection from" what is right, or "overstepping" righteousness. This consistent metaphorical usage has supported the argument that dikê etymologically signifies a line or a directive, and that the word itself should be connected with δείκνυμι and therefore should signify a "mark."[4] Recently, L. R. Palmer has suggested that the word underwent a semantic development from "mark," to "boundary mark," to "judicial decision" (*Trans. Phil. Society* 1950, pp. 149-69). Chantraine prefers the sense of "direction,"[5] but he does not exclude the possibility of dikê as a "boundary mark" (*Dict. étym.*, s.v. δίκη). M. L. West, p. 184, accepts the plausibility of Palmer's view:

> A straight row of markers would be the result of a fair demarcation, while if some of the stones were moved, so as to take in an additional piece of land, the row would be crooked. Σκολιαὶ δίκαι are thus the unjust decisions (*Op.* 269, 250, 264) and ἰθεῖαι δίκαι just ones (*Op.* 225-26; *h. Dem.* 152; cf. *Op.* 7. 224, 230; *Il.* 18. 508).

This question—whether or not the notion of "straightness" and "crooked-ness," which is explicitly attached to dikê (in the *Iliad* as well as in the works cited above), should be traced back to the etymology of the word "dikê"—deserves careful attention. The parallelism we have already noted between crooked verdicts and deflecting words should make us hesitate before we ac-cept imaginary reconstructions such as Palmer's. Though the epithets "straight" and "crooked" are used especially for dikê and only rarely for any expression meaning *logos* (see, for instance, *Od.* 4. 348; *Erga* 262-63), dikê does assume such an epithet when it means "judgment" and when a verb of saying is present, either explicitly or implicitly. For example, in the celebrated judicial scene

forged on the shield of Achilles (*Il.* 18. 497-508), the judges must decide
who is telling the truth: the man who claims he paid the blood ransom or the
one who denies having received it.[6] The elders sit on stones in the holy circle
(ἱερῷ ἐνὶ κύκλῳ), and each in turn gives his verdict or judgment.[7] The two
talents[8] that lie in the middle of the group of elders seem to be a reward for
the judge "who would *say* the straightest "judgment" (508): τῷ δόμεν ὃς
μετὰ τοῖσι δίκην ἰθύντατα εἴποι. No judicial action in a modern sense has to
be performed by judges sitting in a holy circle. Ordinarily, the wrongdoer is
convicted and the penalty agreed upon by both parties.[9] The judges need
only "say in the straightest way the dikê," or the "verdict"; that is, they must
decide whether one party has paid the blood ransom or not. For the dispute
on which the judges must pronounce their verdict has arisen about this one
point, and the people support either one party or the other (ἀμφὶς ἀρωγοί
[502]). When dikê is finally *pronounced* (εἴποι), it will be straight and just
if, indeed, it is true to the facts; otherwise, it will be crooked dikê. This pro-
nouncement (or sentence) will then be enacted, presumably by the authority
of the basileis, for the dikê—because it is only an order, a rule, essentially a
word—must be enforced by action. For instance, Sarpedon "rules Lycia with
his judgments [rules] and his power" (*Il.* 16. 542): . . . Λυκίην εἴρυτο δίκῃσί
τε καὶ σθένεϊ ᾧ. Here dikê and *sthenos* are parallel and stand in opposition,
as do "words" and "deeds" in proverbial expressions. Because of their defenselessness, judgments can be deflected by violence or force:

> οἳ βίῃ εἰν ἀγορῇ σκολιὰς κρίνωσι θέμιστας
> ἐκ δὲ δίκην ἐλάσωσι, θεῶν ὄπιν οὐκ ἀλέγοντες.
> (*Il.* 16. 387-88)

Crooked judgments (σκολιὰς . . . θέμιστας) mean that "justice" (δίκη) has
been driven away. The passage is certainly Hesiodean in tone, and Ehrenberg (p. 69) thought it had been interpolated after the *Erga*.[10] But I believe,
as I intend to demonstrate, that it is a genuinely Homeric passage: its language can be compared with the language of the judicial scene represented on
the shield of Achilles (*Il.* 18. 497)[11] and that of the scene between Menelaos
and Antilochos in *Il.* 23. 573 ff. In the latter passage, Menelaos feels he has
been tricked by Antilochos's reckless move during the chariot race. "My
arete," he says, "is insulted, and my horses are damaged" (βλάψας δέ μοι
ἵππους [23. 571]; and cf. Hes. *Th.* 89: λαοῖς βλαπτομένοις). In fact Antilochos, by deviating from his own path (παρατρέψας ἔχε μώνυχας ἵππους
ἐκτὸς ὁδοῦ, ὀλίγον δὲ παρακλίνας ἐδίωκεν . . . [423-24]), has forced
Menelaos to give way to him; and Menelaos, perceiving the reckless trick,
threatens him: "you will not get the prize without an oath" (441). Consequently, as Antilochos receives the second prize, Menelaos invites the lords

of the Argives to act as judges: "Come on," he says (23. 573 ff.), "judge impartially [literally, "moving in the middle of both of us"] taking no sides" so that people may not consider my claim as a lie:

> Ἀλλ' ἄγετ', Ἀργείων ἡγήτορες ἠδὲ μέδοντες,
> ἐς μέσον ἀμφοτέροισι δικάσσατε, μηδ' ἐπ' ἀρωγῇ,
> μή ποτέ τις εἴπῃσιν Ἀχαιῶν χαλκοχιτώνων·
> "'Ἀντίλοχον ψεύδεσσι βιησάμενος Μενέλαος
> " οἴχεται ἵππον ἄγων, ὅτι οἱ πολὺ χείρονες ἦσαν
> " ἵπποι, αὐτὸς δὲ κρείσσων ἀρετῇ τε βίῃ τε. "

The expression ἐς μέσον has been taken by Hommel (p. 169) to confirm his view that the judge's verdict moves straight between both parties, leaning toward no one. The impartiality of the judges is also stressed in the expression μηδ' ἐπ' ἀρωγῇ (*Il.* 18. 502).

Nothing prevents us from representing the straight way of dikê as a *logos* or sentence which does not lean prejudicially toward either of the contenders but leads, rather, directly to the reality of the facts, to the ascertainment of the truth. Hommel denies, however, that dikê has the task of ascertaining the truth (p. 170); for him, the goal of dikê is only that of satisfying both contenders in some way. He goes further and denies that dikê and truth are connected (p. 177) in Homer and that in Hesiod the connection between the two realms is realized by a specific mention of the reciprocal nouns (p. 177). But in the passage of Homer that we are analyzing, dikê and the realm of truth are connected *expressis verbis*. Menelaos asks his peers to judge; that is, he asks them to pronounce a sentence that will ascertain the truth and will silence the false assumption held by the people, and even by some of the judges. If Menelaos were simply to state the claim that he is the second winner and that the prize belongs to him since Antilochos was tricky, people would regard this claim as a "*lie*":

> Ἀντίλοχον ψεύδεσσι βιησάμενος Μενέλαος
> οἴχεται ἵππον ἄγων. . . .
>
> (*Il.* 23. 576 f.)

They would say, "Menelaos takes the prize because he has the advantage in rank and power, though in reality he lost the game." In the eyes of the people, Menelaos's claim would be a lie, and therefore he would be wrong in claiming victory. Menelaos wants his claim to be found truthful and proclaimed so, in accordance with the reality of the facts; he promises that his claim will be rebuked by no one, for his own verdict will be straight:

> Εἰ δ' ἄγ' ἐγὼν αὐτὸς δικάσω, καί μ' οὔ τινά φημι
> ἄλλον ἐπιπλήξειν Δαναῶν · ἰθεῖα γὰρ ἔσται.
>
> (*Il.* 23. 579-80)

> Come on, I'll give my verdict, and I tell you that
> no Argive will rebuke me, for it will be a straight
> verdict.

In this context the straight verdict will be the true one, pitted against the lie (ψεύδεσσι) of which people might accuse Menelaos. Consequently, Menelaos forces Antilochos to take a solemn oath—as Menelaos had already challenged Antilochos to do—under which Antilochos excuses himself and gives the prize to Menelaos. The straight dikê produced by Menelaos consists in proving the truth of his claim. In proving and publicizing this truth he settles the quarrel.[12] Indeed, Achilles and the Argives do not need to act as judges and to pronounce a regular verdict, simply because Antilochos renounces his claim and his prize. Thus the straight dikê is produced in the form of a truthful statement before the judges and is ascertained as such by the judges. By giving back his prize, Antilochos accepts defeat and shows that his claim was false, for in reality he had tricked Menelaos, deflecting him from his way. (Even the trick used by Antilochos is phrased in such a way as to evoke the deflecting and deviating movement of lies.)[13]

In order to complete the analysis of all the instances of dikê in the *Iliad*, we should look at the passage *Il.* 19. 180 ff., where no verb of speaking occurs and where dikê is not called "straight": the word does not imply a judgment or an arbitration but loosely designates a "rule" or "that which is due."[14] We therefore pass to the *Odyssey*.

Ehrenberg (pp. 58–59) explains why Nestor is said to know the ways (δίκας) and the mind (φρόνιν) of others (*Od.* 3. 244): as Telemachos immediately adds (3. 247), Nestor knows what is true. Ehrenberg continues: "Rechtes und Wahres gehen zusammen, denn das Finden des Wahren liegt in der Tätigkeit des Richter" (p. 59).[15]

All these considerations ought to deter us from jumping to the conclusion that the connections between the notions "straight:crooked" and dikê should be traced back to an "original" meaning of dikê as a straight row of marks or a straight line. For we should also notice that these epithets are not constantly used, but are basically applied to the idea of dikê as *judgment*. Furthermore, we might well consider that in both Romance and Germanic languages the idea of justice/right/Rechts has proceeded from the notion of straight and has neglected the Latin *jus*. Thus French *droit* and Italian *diritto* are traced back to *directum*; and it is not improbable that the metaphor has, again, originated in the realm of the *logos*.[16]

My contention is that the polarity "straight:crooked" applied to dikê need not be explained by an "original" meaning of dikê itself. The Greeks of Homeric times—and of later times—viewed truth in terms of "things as they are." A true *logos* represents things "straightly" or goes through them or to them on a straight path or road, whereas a false *logos* deflects them in various ways. With-

in the framework of this metaphor—which governs the *logos* itself—it is possible
to understand the application of the notions "straight" and "crooked" to the
discourse of dikê. Dikê is the "direction" or "indication" (δείκνυμι) that
becomes "just" when its (judicial) *logos indicates* straightly things as they
are, or moves in the straight direction. What makes this discourse and its tremendous executive force "just" is simply its truth. That is why the determination of its truth often takes the form of an ordeal, oaths, and evidence.

This argument does not preclude the possibility that the judicial *logos*, i.e.,
the "judgment" or "verdict" of dikê, might have extended the metaphors
"straight" and "crooked" to the *logos* in general. I would maintain that the
metaphor can be explained in the realm of *logos*, without going back to
special "original" meanings of dikê. For instance, Hommel's view that dikê
is straight because the decision ("Spruch") of the judge goes right between
the claims of the contestants attributes the straightness to the way of the
logos, of the judicial sentence (Hommel, pp. 169-70). For Hommel this *logos*
does not go straight to the real facts or truth, as I have assumed, but it nevertheless marks a straight line, since it does not lean toward either of the two
contenders. This representation of dikê's way seems to me wrong if it implies that decisions do not ascertain the truth about the contender's claim
but simply end with a "splitting of the difference." It may, however, have
some weight if it only implies that the *logos*, when aiming at the truth or
at the true norm, does not lean prejudicially toward any one of the contenders.

DIKÊ IN HESIOD

Before analyzing the long passage *Erga* 215-75, where Dikê is divinized,
we must add a few words on the meaning of dikê in Hesiod and its relationship to the *logos*.

The exact meaning of dikê, Dikê, or dikai is not easy to determine. In
many cases it is difficult to deny dikê an abstract meaning bordering on the idea
of justice, as we saw in *Erga* 9 (see p. 45). But this abstract and moral meaning, strongly supported by many scholars (see recently Krafft, pp. 77 ff.
and bibliography), is vigorously denied by others (see M. Gagarin, "Dikê
in the *Works and Days*," *Classical Philology* 68 [1973]: 81 ff. and bibliography).

Does dikê mean "justice"? To pose the question in these terms is misleading in many ways, especially because no precise equivalent can exist
between cultures as different as the Hesiodean and ours. Yet we can try
to define the sort of "justice" that Hesiod implies. The connection we
have established between dikê, dikai, and truth suggests a stronger moral

connotation in Hesiod than in Homer, since in Hesiod truth is part of a decisive constellation of moral and religious priorities and values. In fact, the
word dikai is repeatedly accompanied by the attributes "straight" or
"crooked," which refer, as we have seen, to a whole moral code (truth,
memory, sweetness, the Muses, protection of Zeus, etc.) This connotation
is so persistent, and the religious moral context so pervasive, that dikai
almost never implies the neutral or indifferent notion of "decisions";
rather, it implies either "right" or "wrong" decisions and settlements.
As concerns dikê, the word is never termed "crooked," but a few times
it is termed "straight" (*Il.* 18.508, 23. 580; Hes. *Erga* 224, *fr.* 174). In *Erga*
224, dikê is qualified as "not straight," but here dikê is overcome and abused
by the bad kings. The word alone (unless used ironically) always means an act
of justice, whether in the abstract sense (*e.g. Erga* 9. 279) or in the more concrete meaning of "just judgment"–"just reward or punishment."

We might define dikê as the judgment and the norm that is established
from a posture of impartiality and truth before the reciprocity of claims
and that admit only peaceful attitudes in the settlement. The same word,
then, may designate precisely that posture which is often invoked in the
case of Dikê.

At the beginning of the *Erga*, Hesiod bids his brother to avoid the possibility that "Strife, rejoicing in evil, may turn your mind from work." (28).
Perses should, on the contrary, devote himself to agricultural activity, for
only when one has acquired abundance can one indulge in contention and
wrangling. This time Perses will not succeed in contending and wrangling
for others' wealth:

> Let us settle again [(or "here")] our quarrel with straight
> judgments (ἀλλ᾽, αὖθι διακρινώμεθα νεῖκος ἰθείῃσι
> δίκης) from Zeus, which are the best. Already we have
> divided our inheritance, and you have taken and
> seized much besides by largely honoring the gift-
> devouring Basileis who are ready to dispense this kind
> of justice (τήνδε δίκην)! Fools, for they do not
> know how much more is the half than the whole and what
> advantage there is in the mallow and asphodel.

The text contains allusions that are not clear to us, such as the reference to
a legal suit between the two brothers, but the general sense of the passage is
obvious, and the set of values connected with the just decisions and with justice are forcefully stressed.

Perses' and Hesiod's inheritance has been divided in unequal shares,[17] and
Hesiod is apparently asking for a friendly revision of that decision. If the

basileis were inspired by the Muses, as are those of whom Hesiod speaks in
Th. 84 ff., Hesiod might even ask for a legal revision of the past decision. In
this case the basileus would speak unerringly and sweetly, persuading Perses
to return what he had seized in excess of his share. By this restitution (μετάτροπα
ἔργα [*Th*. 89]) the basileus would remove the damage that Hesiod had suffered
at the dealings in the agora, during the legal decision (see λαοῖς βλαπτομένοις
ἀγορῆφι [*Th*. 88-89]). But the tone of the *Erga* passage does not show any
confidence in the straightness, sweetness, and persuasiveness of the basileis.
Hesiod, therefore, speaks in their place and tries to convince Perses that there
is another way to obtain wealth—a just way, protected and supported by Zeus.
This way is the way of dikê. Its straight verdict comes from Zeus (see also *Erga*
9), and the ensuing settlement assures an equal division, according to the rule
of inheritance.

The text is sufficiently vague about Perses' precise seizure: it says only
ἄλλα πολλά. This expression recalls the previous κτήμασ᾽ ἐπ᾽ ἀλλοτρίοις
(33-34). Here the poet concedes that a fully satisfied man, rich in his domain,
might seek others' wealth through contention and wrangling: the poet is probably thinking here of the basileis who receive gifts or of the contenders who,
by offering gifts, obtain the favor of the basileis. But now, the text implies,
Perses will not be able to repeat his first action. We do not know why; the
nature of his first action, however, is clear. He was able to influence the
judges by offering them gifts, and he was therefore able to have them lean
toward him, instead of being in the middle as dikê requires (*Il*. 23. 574).

The quarreling and contention over the wealth of others illustrated by
Perses' seizure of ἄλλα πολλά is an attack on that which is "others'," and
it therefore blurs the reciprocity, or balance, between τὰ ἑαυτοῦ and τὰ ἀλλότρια.
Dikê protects the reciprocal elements contained in these terms. It is, of course,
difficult and problematic in many cases to draw a clear line between the
two realms, but this does not concern Hesiod. The "straight" or "right"
verdicts which come from Zeus would easily identify the two realms in the
actual case of a division of inheritance and would give to Hesiod and Perses what each is really due. In this way, dikê presages somehow the Platonic.
view of justice: τὸ προσῆκον ἑκάστῳ ἀποδιδόναι (*Rep*. I. 332 B-C). By the
same token, the notion of dikê as protector of the line between τὰ ἑαυτοῦ
and τὰ ἀλλότρια helps us to understand why agriculture is, by definition,
"just" (δικαία) in comparison with other activities. It provides goods from the
common mother, Earth, and not through other men. Detienne has elaborated
this point well, quoting in support the authority of Ps. Arist. *Oec*. 1343 a 25 ff:

ἡ δὲ γεωργικὴ μάλιστα ὅτι δικαία· οὐ
γὰρ ἀπ᾽ ἀνθρώπων οὔθ᾽ ἑκόντων ὥσπερ καπηλεία

καὶ μισθαρνικαί, οὔτ᾽ ἀκόντων ὥσπερ αἱ
πολεμικαί.

> Agriculture [conforms to nature] especially because it
> is just, for it does not depend on consenting men, as trade
> and wage earning employments do, nor on unwilling men,
> as war does.

Through agricultural activity, men derive food and wealth from the earth
which nourishes all men; hence agriculture impinges on no one, but thrives
on what is common to everyone.

Dikê implies reciprocity in erotic poetry as well. Here, reciprocity concerns the sentiment of love: injustice (adikia) arises when a lover does not
share the same feeling as his partner (see Theognis 1283 ff.; Sappho I. 20-24
L.P.; Eur. *Med.* 165).[18]

What most characterizes dikê, however, is the peacefulness of its attitude.
The text we are commenting on makes clear the opposition between Eris
κακόχαρτος, and the "erga" of agriculture (28). Analogously, it clarifies the
opposition between νεῖκος, πόλεμος, δῆρις, and ἀγοραί on the one hand and the
straight *dikai* which come from Zeus on the other. The rule of justice is imposed
without violence by a truthful, persuasive, sweet discourse. Similarly, in *Il.* 23.
576 ff., "lie," "force," and "injustice" constitute a whole:

> Ἀντίλοχον ψεύδεσσι βιησάμενος Μενέλαος
> οἴχεται ἵππον ἄγων . . .

People—Menelaos suggests—might think that Menelaos *uses force with lies*
against Antilochos and goes off with the mare [i.e., the prize]. (See also
n. 14, on δίκαιος.) Analogously, when Hesiod describes the reign of total
violence in the second part of the iron age, he sees that justice falls under
the power of might:

> There will be no grace for the man who respects his oath or
> for the just or for the good, but rather men will honor the
> wrongdoer and violence (ὕβριν). Dikê will be in the grasp of
> force, and there will be no reverence. . . .
>
> > (*Erga* 190 ff.)

In the hands of "might," dikê is no longer straight, but captive, as we shall
see in *Erga* 220 ff: for dikê declares the rule by persuasive discourse and not
by any deed of force. Even in the case of Nereus, which we have already witnessed, dikê agrees with a kind, sweet, gentle discourse (*Th.* 233 ff.).

Truly, as Dikê is divinized, she is imagined with some power of action
but she can only send evil to the people whose basileis disregard or insult

her; she can never counteract evil by fighting or even defending herself. Significantly, there is no penal code connected to dikê; dikê is peaceful, and wants to persuade. She is a straight, truthful *logos*, protected by Zeus.

Thus the poet wishes to persuade Perses with his words, which ask for a settlement to their quarrel. As we have surmised, it is probably a question of a friendly settlement rather than a legal one.[19] Therefore the poet develops his song, which is inspired, as is the sweet discourse of the good basileus, by the Muses. His aim is to convince and persuade Perses of the right way to gain wealth and be at peace with the gods. Dikê is therefore associated with the song of the poet. It goes without saying that this innocence and defenselessness of dikê constitute its weakness. Hence the despair of the poet at the recognition of what kind of justice exists in the city (see pp. 69 ff.).[20]

But dikê is also associated with the solitary life in the country that represents Hesiod's ideal. By settling the claims of individuals through persuasive discourse, dikê divides and parts (διακρίνεσθαι) former combatants and then reconciles them, leaving all content (see *Th.* 91-92). The result of this discourse points at the formation of private enclosures where τὰ ἑαυτοῦ are present, inside, at hand (*Erga* 361 ff.), in the house or in the barn. The mingling and gathering of people, especially in the agora or in the meeting place, is not encouraged. Nevertheless, even the agora can be praised when a goddess sits near a good judge (*Th.* 430) or the judge himself looks like a god (*Th.* 91-92). In the *Erga*, however, a work that elicits a more bitter view of life, the agora signifies contention, strife, wrangling, conniving, and the captivity of dikê (*Erga* 28-29, 31 ff., 220 ff.). Thus Hesiod's dikê supports the private enclosures that enjoy the presence of abundance, of the gods, and of truth, rather than the public enclosures where people make common decisions or listen to the words of the basileis. If the word of dikê were able to persuade everyone, the community would be formed of pious, self-contented individuals working and honoring the gods in order to preserve the presence and the plenitude of life within their enclosures. This community would therefore mirror the presence and the plenitude of the golden race, as in fact happens (*Erga* 230 ff.) when Dikê is fully honored: abundance and festivity reign in a miraculous and effortless life, while men do not change from generation to generation (235). A kind of identity is reinstated, and the oak tree is full of acorns on its top and honey in its center (233).[21]

Here we meet again the two crucial images of identity and honey; they vouch for the truth of the Muses' *logos*. The circularity of Hesiod's metaphysics of presence appears therefore in all its coherence and force: justice, by analogy to truth, is viewed as the peaceful repression of differences, as the painless establishment of what is "the self's own," and as the recovery of the original "gift," the plenitude of the Earth.

The works frequently cited in this and the next chapters are the following:

Becker, O. *Das Bild des Weges*. Berlin, 1937. (Hereafter cited as Becker.)
Ehrenberg, V. *Die Rechtsidee im frühen Griechentum*. Leipzig, 1921. (Hereafter cited as Ehrenberg.)
van Groningen, B. A. "Hésiode et Persès." *Mededelingen der Koninklijke Nederlandse Akademie van Wetenschappen, Afd. Letterkunde*. Nieuwe Reeks, Deel 20, n. 6. Amsterdam, 1957. (Hereafter cited as van Groningen.)
Hommel, H. "Wahrheit und Gerechtigkeit." *Antike und Abendland* 15 (1969): 159 ff. (Hereafter cited as Hommel.)
Krafft, F. *Vergleichende Untersuchungen zu Homer und Hesiod*. Göttingen, 1963. (Hereafter cited as Krafft.)
Nicolai, W. *Hesiods Erga: Beobachtungen zum Aufbau*. Heidelberg, 1964.
Wolf, E. *Griechisches Rechtsdenken*. 2 vols. Frankfort, 1950. (Hereafter cited as Wolf, I or II.)

NOTES

1.   For recent discussion of the authenticity of the proem (*Erga* 1-10), see L. Bona Quaglia, *Gli "Erga" di Esiodo* (Turin, 1973), pp. 15 ff, Edwards p. 5 ff.; on its style see, in particular, E. Livrea, "Il proemio degli *Erga* considerato attraverso i vv. 9-10," *Helikon* 6 (1966): 442-75. Livrea demonstrates the Hesiodic quality of the diction in *Erga* 1-10, but, aware of the abstractness of this philological method in deciding the question of authenticity (p. 452), he also offers a learned interpretation of the conceptual links existing between the proem and the rest of the *Erga*.

A few comments of my own on the artistry and artificiality of *Erga* 1-10 follow; the lines show no passive use of formulaic epic diction, but seem to be built by adapting, renewing, and reshaping traditional expressions with great artistry. I am unable to determine the extent to which Hesiod is using traditional ritual material here.

In the first line, the plural of ἀοιδή (ἀοιδῆσιν) is unique in Homer (twenty-five occurrences of the word) and Hesiod (fourteen examples); the expression κλείω ἀοιδῇ (*Th.* 44) or ἀοιδῆσιν (*Erga* 1) offers an exceptional syntactical connection that is alien to Homer, for whom ἀοιδή and κλέος seem interchangeable (G. Nagy, *Comparative Studies in Greek and Indic Meter* [Cambridge, Mass.], pp. 248 ff.). Finally, the participial form κλείουσαι and its position in the verse are unprecedented in Homer.

In line 2 the verb ὑμνέω is not Homeric (for the forms of ὑμνέω, see G.P. Edwards, *The Language of Hesiod in Its Traditional Context* (Oxford, 1971), p. 119); Δία is never elided in Homer, but the elision occurs twice in Hesiod (*Th.* 468 and *Erga* 2).

Line 3 begins with a possible etymological pun on Δία : ὅν τε διά (see the discussion in Bona Quaglia, *Gli "Erga" di Esiodo*, p. 23, n. 17); in line 4 the expression Διὸς μεγάλοιο ἕκητι / may well be traditional: notice the respect of the digamma in ἕκητι and compare *Od.* 20. 42: Διός τε σέθεν τε ἕκητι covering the same portion of the verse.

In line 5 βριάω is not Homeric, though the metrical model of the beginning ῥέα is (*Il.* 17. 461, and see Livrea, "Il proemio," p. 448, n. 24).

The novelty of the metaphorical use of ἀρίζηλον and its fine contrast to ἄδηλον, with a possible play on their common etymological origin (Livrea, "Il proemio," p. 449, n. 20) go along with the fixed position of the word: in Homer ἀρίζηλος occupies this same position in the line five times in seven occurrences of the word. On the "religious associations" of this word see G. P. Shipp, *Studies in the Language of Homer*, 2d ed. (Cambridge: At the University Press, 1972, p. 124.

To the novelty of the metaphorical use of expressions like ἀέξει (6) κάρφει (7), we should add the rarity of ἀγήνορα used here as a noun: only once, in speaking of Achilles, does Homer employ this otherwise common epithet in the same way (*Il.* 9. 699). Also, ὑπέρτατα δώματα in line 9 is unknown to Homer. The position of ἐτήτυμα (10) closing the line is traditional and consistent in all fourteen occurrences of the word in Homer. Yet this traditional trait goes along with the obvious occasionality of naming the brother (Πέρσῃ; on the dative, see Livrea, "Il proemio," pp. 455 ff.), and with the shocking contrast of τύνη (You, Zeus) with ἐγώ δέ (I) in lines 9-10 (see ibid, pp. 455 ff.).

2.   Θέμιστες is found five times in the *Iliad*, and it means, variously, "Gebote, Sprüche, and Weisungen" (Wolf I, p. 73), i.e., "commands," "verdicts" (or "judgments"), "directives."

3.   ταῦτα δ᾽ ἅ μ᾽ εἰρωτᾷς καὶ λίσσεαι, οὐκ ἄν ἐγώ γε
      ἄλλα παρὲξ εἴποιμι παρακλιδόν, οὐδ᾽ ἀπατήσω.

On these lines, see p. 10, on παρέξ, see M. Leumann, *Homerische Wörter*, (Basel, 1950), p. 96 ff. Παρεκ appears as a preverb in Hes. *Erga* 226: καὶ μή τι παρεκβαίνουσι δικαίου. Another example of this notion of "deviation" is *Od.* 19. 555-56, which reads: ὄνειρον ἄλλῃ ἀποκλίναντ᾽.

4.   "Il est clair que le terme est apparenté à δείκνυμι "montrer" "désigner" (δικεῖν ne peut être rapproché que dans la mesure où c'est un développement

particulier du thème de δείκνυμι)" (Chantraine, *Dict. étym.*, s.v. δίκη). cf. Hommel, p. 168.

5.   See K. Latte, "Das Rechtsgedanke im archaischen Griechentum," *Antike und Abendland* 2 (1946): 65: "Es (δίκη) scheint zunächst das Weisen einer Richtung bedeutet zu haben" (i.e., the *pointing out of a direction*). See also Latte's bibliography. The pointing out of a direction also means "the pointing out of a line along which the 'right' conduct must move." Hence the meaning of δίκη as "manner," "way." (*Od.* 4. 691; 14. 59; 19. 43; 24. 255, etc.) V. Ehrenberg favors the other traditionally proposed etymology: δίκη from δικεῖν, "to throw." This etymology is upheld by making δίκη "the throw," one form of ordeal. Whether the throw is straight or crooked and whether or not the thrower hits ἐς μέσον, determines whether the gods will accede to a claim or not. But this and the rest of the assumptions by Ehrenberg, though ingenious, are made without sufficient evidence to support them.

6.   On the alternative meanings, see Ehrenberg, p. 55 n. 2, who translates this passage as I do, and P. Chantraine, *Grammaire homérique*, vol. 2, pp. 310 and 335, where the possible alternative translation is given as "one promised to pay everything and the other refused to accept."

7.   On lines 497–508 see L. Gernet, "Droit et prédroit dans la Grèce ancienne," in *Année Sociologique 1948-49*, pp. 70–76.

8.   Ch. Picard, *Mélanges H. Grégoire*, vol. 1 (Brussels, 1949) "Sur le travail poétique d' Homère," pp. 489–502, brilliantly reconstructs a layer of the epic tradition of this passage in which the τάλαντα are the scales. Detienne, pp. 37 ff., has received this assumption favorably. But the brilliance of Picard's insight is not sufficiently supported. His view that in other passages of the *Iliad* there are equivocations between scales and golden bars is not convincing: τάλαντα in the *Iliad* mean golden bars and are used as prizes or values (M. Leumann, *Homerische Wörter*, pp. 282 ff.). Picard's hypothesis seems therefore only remotely plausible.

9.   That the judges establish neither a culprit nor a punishment, but simply whether or not an action has been performed, might suggest that the scene represents an act of arbitration. But see the objections in Gernet, "Droit et prédroit."

10.   See Krafft, p. 77, for other bibliography.

11.   For *Il.* 16. 387: βίῃ σκολιὰς κρίνωσι θέμιστας. See also *Il.* 23. 576: Ἀντίλοχον ψεύδεσσι βιησάμενος Μενέλαος (Menelaos, using his higher position, would appear to use violence—through lies—on Antilochos.) For the whole question, see chapter 3, pp. 67 ff. and p. 79 n. 21.

12.   Hommel notes that this case, too, ends in a compromise as does *Il.* 18. 497-508 and *Th.* 84 ff. M. Gagarin, "Dikê in the *Works and Days*," *Classical Philology* 68 (1973): 85 thinks that the purpose of the trial in *Il.* 18. 497-

508 is "to find the best compromise." But in these two cases the idea of a compromise is only a possible assumption. In the case of Menelaos and Antilochos, the straight dikê ends, in my view, with the recognition that Menelaos's claim is true and right. The prize belongs, therefore, to Menelaos (591, 609-10). If Menelaos then leaves the prize to Antilochos, this gesture is not necessarily connected with the straight dikê but rather with the heroic code of honor and alliance (see 606-8) and with Menelaos's paternalistic attitude toward the young Antilochos (see 605). On the other hand, I agree that in most cases the judges would not be able to ascertain the truth and would probably try some form of compromise. But the straight dikê in this passage of Homer must mean a truthful one; and Hesiod would not trouble the Muses and Zeus to inspire the judges with less than truth (*Th.* 94, 96).

13.   Becker views "the crooked words" of *Erga* 262 as a metaphor from racing (p. 86). In *Il.* 23. 424, during the chariot race, Antilochos cheats Menelaos by turning from his "right way" and dangerously pressing his adversary. The metaphor of the "way" or "road" is certainly very important for the *logos*. A *logos* is like a "being" that goes through things (*Il.* 9. 56, 61) and reaches a *telos* (*Il.* 19. 107), which is a goal or a place. A *logos* that does not keep to its own way can be said to decline, to cheat, to be false. This view complements the one that I have presented. On the relationship between οἴμη ("subject matter") of the epos and οἶμος ("way," "path"), see A. Pagliaro "Aedi e rapsodi" in *Saggi di critica semantica* (Messina and Florence, 1953), pp. 34 ff. He presents a new etymology and explanation for both expressions.

A pioneering paper on the way the logos "walks" is M. Durante's "Epea pteroenta. La parola come "cammino" in immagini greche e vediche," *Rendiconti dell' Accademia Nazionale dei Lincei*, Classe di scienze morali, storiche e filologiche, Series 8ᵃ, vol. 13 (Rome, 1958), pp. 3 ff.

14.   In *Il.* 19. 180-81 (quoted below), δίκη could mean also Achilles' claim, or what is due to him. Thus, for instance, Wolf's and Ehrenberg's rendering of "Anspruch" or "Anrecht."

> . . . ἵνα μή τι δίκης ἐπιδευὲς ἔχῃσθα.
> Ἀτρεΐδη, σὺ δ᾽ ἔπειτα δικαιότερος καὶ ἐπ᾽ ἄλλῳ
> ἔσσεαι.

But δικαιότερος in line 181 makes better sense if δίκη means simply the "practice" or "rule" that governs the settlement of a quarrel: otherwise Agamemnon would be δικαιότερος only if δίκη meant both Achilles' claim *and* a just claim, i.e., one compatible with the rules of the settlement.

Analogously, in *Il.* 23. 542, which reads, Πηλεΐδην Ἀχιλῆα δίκη ἡμείψατ᾽ ἀναστάς, Antilochos turns to Achilles, "appealing to the *rules* of the game, to *justice*." But this line could also mean "appealing to his own right, his own claim," for the rules attribute to him, as the second racer, a certain right.

Krafft interprets δίκη in *Od.* 14. 84 as "custom," "rule," "practice" (p. 77).

Δίκαιος appears in the *Iliad* with the meaning "fair," "reasonable," "opposed to violence": see *Il.* 16. 542, where dikê is opposed to *sthenos*. On that word, see Krafft, pp. 77 ff.

15. See also Detienne, p. 33: ". . . dans la pensée religieuse, la justice n'est un domain distinct de la verité."

16. *Th. L.L.*: "*Directum* i.q. rectum iustum, Itala, *Psalm*, 19.9: iura domini directa (δικαιώματα εὐθέα; Vulg. iustitiae rectae). Gregor. Tur. *h.F.* 3. 7 *ecce verbum directum habemus.*"

The whole passage is:

Nunc autem Herminefredus quod mihi pollicitus est
fefellit et omnino haec adimplire dissimulat.
Ecce verbum directum habemus: Eamus cum dei
adiuturio contra eos.

See also M. Bonnet, *Le Latin de Grégoire de Tours*, (Paris, 1890), p. 280: "Le juste est comparé à la ligne droite; *directus, directum* commence à prendre le sens qu'il a en français, droit, le droit. *Ecce verbum directum habemus* dit Thierry à ses Francs en marchant contre Hermenefred *h.F.* 3, 7 p. 115, 2, nous avous le bon droit pour nous, mot à mot, la parole juste. Au contraire, Clotaire, pour déturner les siens d'une guerre injuste contre les Saxons, s'écrie: *verbum directum non habemus, h.F.* 4,14 p. 152, 3."

The English "right" and the German "Recht" are equivalent to the Latin *rēctus* (for *rĕctus*), meaning "straight," "right."

17. For the purpose of defining Hesiod's view of justice it does not make a great deal of difference whether Perses actually gets more than his share or whether he simply tries to, and the judges turn down his claims. Van Groningen has defended this last view with a forceful interpretation of the whole passage. Yet his idea that the suit has been adjudicated with an unfavorable result for Perses raises many questions and is grounded on elusive evidence. In the first place, if the judges really recognize Hesiod's legitimate claim, his invective against the judges becomes incomprehensible: "Fools! for they do not know how much more is the half than the whole . . . (40–41)." Furthermore, the epithet δωροφάγος has most certainly a pejorative connotation: see δημοβόρος *Il.* 1. 231. Analogously, Hesiod's endless attack against the judges in the *Erga* would be senseless, especially if we recall how highly he esteems the good judges in the *Theogony*.

Secondly, van Groningen builds his evidence on the imperfect ἐφόρεις (*Erga* 38), interpreting it as a conative imperfect. Perses therefore "tried" to seize much beside his share. But even if we should absolutely grant this connotation of the imperfect, it does not follow that the attempt was vain. The imperfect might represent the long efforts of Perses to convince and bribe the judges, and it might reflect the various phases of the trial: it might border on an imperfect of duration.

But neither of these senses is necessary. In Homer the imperfect has often a sense close to that of the aorist (Chantraine, *Gram. homér.*, vol. 2, pp. 190, 193 ff.); and in Hesiod, too, the imperfect is used in parallel performance to the aorist apparently without substantial difference: see for instance στέφον (*Erga* 75), ἔμμνε (*Erga* 96, which is the reading of all MSS.), etc.

18.   See B. Gentili, "Il 'letto insaziato' di Medea e il tema dell' adikia," *Studi classici e orientali* 21 (1972) 60 ff.

19.   It is improbable that the basileis would review their previous decision. Van Groningen also assumes that Hesiod would appeal to Perses to desist from trying a new legal action.

20.   The interpretation of δίκη in these two passages is disputed (see Nicolai, p. 23, n. 20).

21.   On the utopia of the City of Justice, see M. Gigante, "La città dei giusti in Esiodo e gli Uccelli di Aristofane," *Dioniso*, 11 (1948): 20, where he describes the "ethic and religious zeal" that sustains this ideal.

In showing correspondences between the golden age and the City of Justice I agree with Bona Quaglia, *Gli "Erga" di Esiodo*, p. 143.

Chapter 3

DIKÊ, THE GODDESS

Dans les "anthropomorphismes" par quoi se
constitue la pensée metaphysique il n'y a
pas de notion éthique qui ait eu autant
d'importance que celle du δίκαιον.

L. Gernet, *Droit et societé
dans la Grèce ancienne*

If Hesiod did not divinize Dikê,[1] he is certainly the author responsible for
her Olympian status, who gave her both a pedigree and a precise mythical
background. The divinization occurs in the *Theogony* (901 ff.) and in *Erga*
(256 ff.), where Hesiod gives a genealogical account of Dikê. The latter passage, along with that which precedes and follows it, is an exciting piece of
poetry, and in it we see formed the powerful metaphysical notion of Justice.

Hesiod's account (λόγος [106]) of the metal ages ends with the gloomy
prophecy that the present iron age will decline into an age even worse.[2] At
this juncture the text returns to the present (νῦν [202]) and recounts a fable
(αἶνος) for the kings, wise men that they are (φρονέουσι καὶ αὐτοῖς).[3] It is
the fable of the hawk and the nightingale (*Erga*, 202-212). Its general meaning is that it is foolish for the weak to bewail or protest against the violence of
the powerful; for in resisting injustice the weak receive injury as well as ridi-
cule. The fable, explicitly addressed to the basileis, reads as follows:

> Poor thing, why do you cry out? One far stronger
> than you holds you fast (ἔχει νύ σε πολλὸν ἀρείων
> [207]), and you shall go where I take you (τῇ δ᾽ εἷς,
> ἧ σ᾽ ἂν ἐγώ περ ἄγω [208]) though you are a singer
> (ἀοιδόν); and I'll make my meal of you or let you go, as
> it pleases me. The person who wants to fight against more
> powerful people is a fool; he is both deprived of victory
> (νίκης τε στέρεται [211]) and suffers pain besides scorn.[4]

61

The moral of the story, as the hawk tells it, resembles the kind of moral that the bribed basileis might like to apply to Hesiod and his poetry. For the story of the nightingale, who is the singer pierced by the curved talons (γναμπτοῖσι . . . ὀνύχεσσι [205]) of the hawk, constitutes a transparent metaphor for Hesiod's protest throughout the *Erga* against the crooked verdicts of the basileis.

There can be little doubt that the nightingale/singer and the hawk refer to Hesiod and the basileis, respectively. The word ἀοιδός cannot evoke anything else but the "professional poet": in the whole epic *corpus* (in which we find about fifty occurrences of the word) ἀοιδός consistently designates the poet, the professional singer (see Pagliaro, pp. 5 ff.). Only in line 25 (interpolated?) of the *Hymn to Hermes* is the word used as an adjective (χέλυν . . . ἀοιδόν), but here, too, it refers to the poetic activity, since it qualifies the tortoise.5

The poet, therefore, marks the fable with his own signature: the nightingale (ἀηδών) is the poet (ἀοιδός); so Hesiod appropriates the melodious song of the nightingale and its desperate situation. Far from singing the truthful song that the Muses teach him in a sacred precinct and aloof from men, here Hesiod signs as his own a song that is no magic gift, but a lament and a protest against injustice and violence.

This song, then—the poem we are listening to—fruitless as it may be in the basileis' judgment, is not an instinctive, animal response on the part of the nightingale/poet; it is, on the contrary, an unmistakable commitment to fight a real battle against the powerful, as the verb ἀντιφερίζειν (210) confirms in this context.6

The voice of the poet is, therefore, superimposed on to that of the nightingale; Hesiod disturbs the objectivity of his *ainos* in order to express a personal commitment. Likewise, though more explicitly, in the previous passage on the races Hesiod has violated the objectivity of his "logos" and uttered the personal wish that he had not been born during the fifth age of iron, but that he "might have died in a preceding age or lived in a following one." (174-75). The personal tone introduced into the two situations invites us to investigate the relationship between the two passages. This last passage (174-75) is a bit cryptic, and it is probably hazardous to try to extend the meaning of the text and ask it to signify more than, "Oh, would that I had not been born in this age!" Yet I am tempted to interpret these lines as a reference to another, specific age.

The age that immediately precedes Hesiod's is the heroic age, which is blessed; it is especially blessed for those heroes who, after death, inhabit the Isles of the Blessed. As a poet, Hesiod might then have sung the "glory of the gods and of the heroes" instead of a song of pity (ἐλεόν [205]).7 Nevertheless, it is unlikely that Hesiod would have liked to have been a poet like Homer or a hero like Achilles. There can be no doubt, however, about what age Hesiod would have preferred and what function Hesiod would have liked to fulfill.

Since he saw the silver and bronze ages as too negative, Hesiod would have embraced the golden age; the life of the people at that time was entirely good (116), and at death they became immortal guardians on behalf of Dikê (*Erga* 122 ff. and 252 ff.). This certainly sounds like an ideal profession for Hesiod: to serve Dikê as an immortal daimon, not as a farmer-poet who risks both scorn and defeat in his fight against Hybris.

It is less difficult to guess which future age Hesiod might have wanted to live in, since only one age follows the fifth. The so-called sixth age, the gloomiest of all, is almost the inverse of the golden age. Yet, with all its misery, this age has only one dimension—no contrast between black and white. No Justice, no *aidos*, will survive. Justice will reside only in physical strength (i.e., in violence [192]). There will be no *defense* or *remedy* against evil (201). No *logos* will oppose Hybris; no *logos*, gift of the Muses, will sweetly divert men's minds from their pains. Poetry will not exist; there will be no fight against evil, for there will be no good to oppose it.

Hesiod's present position, on the contrary, is that of a fighter for justice in the world of Hybris; for only in the iron age, Hesiod's age, can good *and* evil coexist (179): ἀλλ' ἔμπης καὶ τοῖσι μεμείξεται ἐσθλὰ κακοῖσιν. The polarity "good:bad" is explicitly mentioned only in the iron age. The golden age is totally good (ἐσθλὰ τὰ πάντα [116]); the silver age is shadowy and basically negative; the bronze age gleams with weapons and is suicidal (152); the fourth age, that of the heroes, while more just than the previous one (158), contains wars that take the heroes to death or to the Isles of the Blessed; the last age, after the present iron age, will be totally bad. Thus only Hesiod's age, the fifth age, is characterized by the balance good:bad.

In the present age, therefore, Hesiod knows not only the violence of injustice but also the presence of Dikê—not only the crooked judgments but also the straight ones. The uncertain outcome of the fight for Justice prompts the longing of 174 ff. and the bitter remark at 270–71; nevertheless, Hesiod assumes as his goal the amplification and strengthening of Dikê's protesting voice. Though at first glance the fable of the hawk and the nightingale seems to support a cynically realistic attitude toward power and brutality, it contains, on closer examination, opposition to such an attitude, when it is seen in connection with the ideas that we have suggested. While the fable seems to end with a moral favorable to the powerful basileis, it nevertheless presents a voice that, although weak, struggles against these lords and is foolish (ἄφρων) enough to challenge those in power, with their realistic wisdom (φρονέουσι [202]). Another set of polarities emerges from behind the two subjects of this story:

hawk	:	nightingale
basileis	:	Hesiod

strong words	:	lament (μύρετο [206])
"		song (ἀοιδός [208])
force, power	:	defenselessness, suffering
wisdom (*Erga* 202;	:	foolishness
Th. 88)		

The two columns of terms are not, as they now stand, altogether complete: it is impossible, for instance, to assign the polarity "good:bad," since no ethical evaluation of the hawk's teaching is offered. However, the fable does establish the hawk's position as both reasonable and realistic. It is, therefore, foolish for the poet/nightingale to fight a battle against the basileis/hawk. Nevertheless, foolish though this attempt may appear to the basileis, the battle is fought, and the hero of the battle is Hesiod, with his *logos.* The metaphorical elements of the fable will indeed displace the terms of the conflict, through a process of "metaphorization" or displacement that will lead to the final victory of Dikê. At the very beginning of the fable, the nightingale is represented as being at once a powerless victim and a struggling warrior. Already, this contradictory representation illustrates the process of displacement that the *logos* elicits, provoking all sorts of ambiguities in the text. Hesiod will not be able to change the social structure in which he is a poet/nightingale and the basileis are all-powerful and arrogant. But while the basileis and the hawk cannot be socially and ethically transformed, the poet will be able to reverse other polarities. The poet's song will become powerful enough to command Zeus's attention, an event that presents us with an ambiguity, since the basileis descend from Zeus and are especially protected by him (*Th.* 96).

The encounter between the hawk and the nightingale appears, in the words of the hawk, as a *struggle* between them. The nightingale seems foolish for protesting and resisting (ἀντιφερίζειν implies a rivalry between heroes or gods) and, as if this were a struggle between two heroes or gods, for being so bold as to fight for victory. The poet immediately identifies the heroes or daimons of this struggle by turning to his brother Perses and urging him to harken to Justice (Dikê) and not to support Hybris (213): Ὦ Πέρση, σὺ δ᾽ ἄκουε δίκης, μηδ᾽ ὕβριν ὄφελλε. Though most editors and interpreters assume that Dikê and Hybris are inanimate, I believe that we should here understand them to be the names of the personified Dikê and Hybris, for ἀκούω, in the sense of "obey," or "hearken to," implies response to a speaking person, a voice.[8] Furthermore, the two verbs, ἀκούω and ὀφέλλω exactly suit attributes that, though related to the nightingale and the hawk, could be transferred to Dikê and Hybris: "Perses, harken to Dikê and do not foster Hybris." The voice of Dikê is Hesiod's song of the nightingale's protest and of its fight (ἀντιφερίζειν) against the hawk. The voice of the poet, then, coming from the Muses, animates the lament of the nightingale, imagines that the hawk/basileis recognizes it as a fighting voice, and finally defines itself as the voice of Dikê.

On the other hand, the hawk/basileis does have power: the verb ὀφέλλω is an appropriate expression of this attribute, since in Homer it is often used in the sense of increasing or intensifying force, power, fatigue, etc.[9]

As some scholars have noticed,[10] Hesiod's plea for Perses to harken to justice and his faith that Dikê will prevail in the end (217-18) constitute the poet's immediate answer to the moral teaching of the hawk.[11] First, Hybris is bad, not only for poor people,[12] but also for the powerful man whom it burdens: "It [Hybris] is as serious for him as a wound and sits clearly upon his neck as a Daimon. Man is thought of as going his way and the Daimon rides him, and weighs upon him so that he runs directly to his ruin" (Becker, p. 87). (See also *Il.* 16. 519: βαρύθει δέ μοι ὦμος ὑπ αὐτοῦ.) It is better to follow the other road, that which leads to Justice,[13] as a fool learns by experience (218).

The image of the road is important: it governs the next passages and it explains why Dikê does not now appear as the prevailing daimon. Only when the whole way has been traveled can Dikê clearly prevail, but the length of the journey cannot be foreseen.

As the *logos* increasingly rearranges the terms of the conflict and "metaphorizes" the situation, its claim of representing the stability of truth becomes more evident. In this case, Dikê is transformed from an animal in a fable to a goddess and assumes her own assured place. Although the hawk and the nightingale have a bloody encounter in mid-air, and the nightingale is drawn up toward the clouds (204), no encounter at all now takes place between Dikê and Hybris. What begins as a massacre by the hawk is soon transformed into a heroic struggle; it then becomes a contest in which one of the contenders has the better way (κρείσσων [217]) and is therefore destined for victory.

The two roads lie apart: Hybris's probably runs to the left and Dikê's to the right.[14] Thus the text conjures up another polarity—that of *arete* (virtue, excellence) and *kakotes* (vice, baseness). This polarity is characterized by two roads: one, difficult; the other, easy (*Erga* 287 ff.). Eventually, however, the road of virtue becomes the easier road (291-92), just as Dikê's road does when she finally prevails (ἐς τέλος [218]).

But in the next lines Dikê's position on her road is again displaced. We see Dikê in the turmoil of random movement, through an image closely parallel to that of the nightingale:

> For Horkos runs suddenly along with crooked judgments.[15]
> And there is a grumbling, when Dikê is dragged away
> where men who devour gifts and give verdicts with crooked

judgments take her ($\tilde{\eta}$ κ'ἄνδρες ἄγωσι [220]). And she
follows, weeping for the city and for the quarters of
people,[16] wrapped in mist and bringing mischief to men
who pushed her forth and did not impart straight judgment.
                                                          (219-24)

The above passage describes Dikê's position as a defenseless daimon on the
roads and paths of men, prey to the powerful. As Dikê is dragged away
wherever men take her, a *rhothos* rises. Commentators are divided in their
opinions of the passage; they interpret it either as "men grumble as they
see Justice opposed by crooked verdicts," or "Justice laments as she is
dragged away." Both interpretations are possible, and both involve some
difficulty. That Dikê laments is certain, for this fact is repeated (κλαίουσα
[222]), while "men's" grumbling could be derived only from the particular
metaphor of " 'rhothos' " describing "the rushing of the surge of the oar"
(Frisk, s.v., ῥόθος), a metaphor that might describe various sounds or noises.
Since, however, Dikê's reacting cry might be a shriek, as some commentators
imply, but more accurately a weeping noise (222), the word "rhothos" can
appropriately be attributed to her.[17]

Just as the nightingale is dragged wherever the hawk wants it to go
($\tilde{\eta}$ σ' ἄν ἐγώ περ ἄγω [208]), so is Dikê dragged wherever powerful
men want her to be taken ($\tilde{\eta}$ κ'ἄνδρες ἄγωσι [222]). And exactly as
the nightingale laments (μύρετο [206]) and fights back (ἀντιφερίζειν [210]),
so, too, does Dikê weep (κλαίουσα [222]) and fight back (κακὸν φέρουσα
[223]). Such parallel actions should be sufficient proof of the rigorous nature
of the analogy: the oppression of the nightingale, of Hesiod, and of Dikê involves the same essential terms—lament/song, defenselessness, suffering and
resistance, traveling on the path or road chosen by the "other," at the will
and whim of the "other." Dikê is invisible (223); but her voice, like the
voice of the poet, can be heard bewailing the wrongs that befall man. The
parallelism also applies to the other terms of the structure, the hawk and the
basileis. Both drag their prey wherever they want, and both persecute Dikê
(224). The hawk and the basileis are both characterized by whims and desires associated with hunger or gluttony.[18] As the hawk pierces his victim
with his curved nails, so do the basileis drive Dikê away with their crooked
judgments.

In the process of becoming a daimon, Hesiod's voice has not merely acquired
new traits: it now faces a different enemy. The basileis are wise (202), and the
hawk is right to treat the nightingale as a fool (ἄφρων [210]), since it is destined to defeat and scorn. But now these same basileis have been degraded to
the ranks of men (ἄνδρες [220], ἄνθρωποι [223]). While they are still basi-

leis inasmuch as they are judges, their previous wisdom has been replaced by crooked judgments. Crookedness is part of the whole parallel structure encompassing, as we have come to understand, lies, forgetfulness, and baseness. This structure stands in direct opposition to the portraits of the good king/judge and Nereus *Th.*, 81 ff. and 233 ff. The just basileus is honored by the Muses, daughters of Zeus (*Th.* 81). The crooked basileis are, however, not honored either by Dikê, daughter of Zeus, by the Muses, or by Zeus himself, as they are Zeus's enemies. This portrait of the basileis seems odd, since the basileis are said to descend from Zeus (*Th.* 96), but the reticence of the text allows such a reading: by "deturning" a little crookedly, the text avoids giving these judges the title of kings and indirectly assumes that they are not honored by Zeus (223-24, 229, 238-39).

Finally, Horkos, the oath, is the ally of Dikê. Horkos is a god, too, a son of Eris (Discord); and his brothers and sisters are Forgetfulness (Λήθη), Battles, Murders, Lies (Ψεύδεα) and *Logoi* (Λόγους) (*Th.* 226 ff.). Horkos punishes those mortals who commit perjury (*Th.* 231 f.; *Erga* 804); therefore here, too, the text should imply that Horkos comes upon crooked, false judgments to pursue them, just as Ate in *Il.* 9. 512 comes upon the sinner to punish him (τῷ [the sinner] ἄτην ἄμ᾽ ἕπεσθαι, ἵνα βλαφθεὶς ἀποτίσῃ). Yet the Hesiodean expression is vague.

The men who give crooked judgments are thus represented in a very harsh light: they resemble, in some ways, the ravagers of cities who despoil the temples of the gods. A powerful set of interrelated moral and religious principles and daimons condemns them to the side of the evil and the unjust. Yet these judges still control the roads and the paths of men, on which Dikê, though invisible, is made captive by the kings. The doublet "Dikê:dikai"[19] is emphasized in lines 220-21, where Dikê is dragged as a captive person,[20] into the agora, where men render unjust dikai (judgments) while Horkos intervenes. The daimonic, hectic activity on the road to the city distinguishes this passage from the Iliadic one (16. 386-88) that Hesiod certainly has in mind. The neatness and the logic of the Homeric passage should be recalled to understand Hesiod's text:

> Ζεύς, ὅτε δὴ ἄνδρεσσι κοτεσσάμενος χαλεπήνῃ,
> οἳ βίῃ εἰν ἀγορῇ σκολιὰς κρίνωσι θέμιστας,
> ἐκ δὲ δίκην ἐλάσωσι, θεῶν ὅπιν οὐκ ἀλέγοντες·
>   (*Il.* 16. 386-88)

> Zeus, angry with men who impart crooked
> verdicts with violence in the assembly and drive
> justice out, caring nothing for the gods' visitation.

Hesiod replaces Homer's precise mention of the "agora" by a relative clause, "where . . . men judge. . . ." In the Homeric text it is clear that when men produce crooked verdicts (θέμιστας), they drive Dikê away from the agora. But Hesiod wants to create a shocking clash using the name Dikê and the dikai to designate justice on the one hand and injustice on the other: he therefore has Dikê dragged as a captive to the agora, where unjust verdicts (σκολιῆς δίκης) are pronounced. Later (224), he picks up the Homeric image of Dikê as she is being dragged away, but at this point the movement of Dikê stands in an unclear relationship with the text that precedes it. One can vaguely understand that Dikê is driven away from her paths as she is captured and as the crooked *dikai* and the crooked judgments take place.[21]

The Hesiodean text conjures up a violent movement along the roads of the city, a dramatic encounter of daimons, the figure of a captive woman, and the sound of her voice as she cries. Yet the more noisy, hectic, and dramatic the encounter sounds, the less serious or bloody are its results for Dikê. First, she is wrapped in mist and is therefore protected by her invisibility; second, although she may be dragged into slavery like a prisoner of war, she is still capable of retaliation by bringing mischief to men. Again the contradiction involved in the idea of a voice that fights back (like the nightingale's in the fable) is reproduced in the image of a captive slave who moves Zeus to act in unprecedented ways. For Zeus provides the city inhabited by those who respect Dikê with the blessings of the golden age (225-37),[22] while the city of those who support Hybris (238) is treated by Zeus as though it were in the final and worst age of man.

By describing the fates of these cities, the text conjures up an alliance between Dikê and Zeus and suggests that it is through Zeus that Dikê possesses her power. The step toward the final goal is simple:

> O basileis, you too should think about this Dikê.[23]
> For the immortals are close to men—indeed, among them—
> and observe all those who harm each other by
> crooked dikai [judgments] , and who disregard the eyes
> (ὄπιν) of the gods.[24] For upon the bounteous
> Earth there are thrice ten thousand immortal watchers of
> mortal men, appointed by Zeus; these keep watch on the
> dikai [judgments] and the wrong deeds as they roam
> wrapped in mist all over the Earth. Present is
> Virgin Dikê (Justice), daughter of Zeus,[25] who is
> honored and respected by the gods who dwell on
> Olympus. And whenever someone hurts her[26] with
> crooked insults she sits immediately beside her

father, Zeus, son of Kronos, and sings him the mind
of unjust men (γηρύετ' ἀνθρώπων ἀδίκων νόον)
until the *demos* pays for the foolishness of the
basileis who, evil-minded, deflect the *dikai* by
speaking crookedly. Keep watch against all this,
you basileis who devour gifts; make straight your
words (μύθους) and forget altogether the crooked
dikai. The man who prepares evil for another man
prepares it for himself; and the evil plan is most
harmful for him who devises it. The eye of Zeus
sees all, understands all, and sees these things
even now, if so he wishes, nor will he fail to mark (οὐδέ ἑ
λήθει) what kind of justice (δίκην) the city holds within it.
Now, then, may neither I nor my son be just (δίκαιος)
among men, since it is bad (κακόν) to be just when
the more unjust obtains greater share [or "justice"]
(δίκην).27 But I do not believe that wise Zeus will
accomplish these things.

(248-73)

In analyzing this passage, we shall pay special attention to two points:
(1) the refinement of the metaphysical formulation of Dikê and the conse-
quent reversal of some of the polarities implicit in the fable; and (2) Hesiod's
logos as the *logos* of Justice (Dikê).

The fundamental theme of struggle that the fable posits is also found here.
But how changed are the characters in this conflict! Even the space involved in
this struggle has become so large that it embraces heaven and earth. The tone
takes on a loftier ring, and we hear one of Hesiod's greatest passages.28

Let us survey the characters. The judges are now people who "wear each
other out (ἀλλήλους)" with their crooked dikai. This statement is new and
striking, and it anticipates the astonishing ethical principle (265-66) that the
man who plans evil for another person harms himself. The basileis have lost the
privileges of the hawk, who can harm the nightingale without harming itself.
For both the basileis and their people (261), punishment is certain, even if the
prospect does not concern them. (251).29 But if the basileis do not care about
divine punishment, if they do not know that they are wounding each other,
they can no longer be called wise. On the contrary, they resemble the drunken
suitors of the *Odyssey* who are likely to wound each other with their weapons
(*Od.* 16. 293 = 19. 12).

In one stroke, therefore, the basileis have lost the impunity and wisdom that
characterized them during the telling of the fable. There are sufficient grounds

to wonder if they are still strong enough to carry away their prey or to
capture Dikê. They seem unable to do so. Now they are characterized not by
powerful hands but simply by hybristic voices. They offend Dikê "with crooked
insults" (σκολιῶς ὀνοτάζων [258]); and they speak crookedly when they de-
viate from the truth or from Dikê (262); they are, therefore, urged to correct
their crooked judgments (264) by straightening their words (263). They still
devour gifts, and this trait becomes even more derogatory in their revised
portrait.

We now see the basileis as fools, throwing insults at a goddess at the risk of
hurting themselves, their peers, and their people. Their power is limited to the
exercise of their voices—crooked, deflecting voices, which insult and harm the
gods. Against this insolent sound stands a bulwark of powerful daimons and
gods: the thirty thousand immortals of the golden age, who keep a watchful
eye as they roam the earth; Dikê, the daughter of Zeus, who commands respect from all gods, including her father; and Zeus himself, who sees everything.

The message here is redundant. The punishment of the basileis has too many
instigators. First, the basileis harm each other simply by saying what they say;
secondly, each harms himself by plotting evil for others; thirdly, the watchers
act against them since they are not merely "observers," but doers, and can, for
instance, bestow riches (*Erga* 126). Finally, Zeus can punish them. Dikê functions
as an informer and, in particular, as a persuader; although, as we shall see, there
is no need for her if Zeus really sees and hears everything or if the kings really
do harm themselves with their own words.

As a result of this new description, the series of polarities that characterized
the encounter between the basileis and Hesiod in the crude allegory of the
fable must undergo a change. While the basileis remain kingly and all-powerful
in the social hierarchy, the metaphysical enhancement of Justice and the various metamorphoses of the conflict describe a new reality:

basileis	:	Hesiod
Hybris	:	Dikê
		Zeus
		Horkos
		30,000 daimons
crooked logos	:	straight logos
suffering, punishment	:	golden age
foolishness (248, 261)	:	wisdom (273)
bad	:	good

As anticipated, the most striking feature of this new set of polarities consists
in the reduction of the real conflict to an encounter of *logoi*. On discounting
the daimonic and the divine characters, one sees that the only conflicting

terms left are two *logoi*—one crooked, foolish, and bad, the other straight, wise, and good. That Hesiod believes in the reality of the divine and daimonic characters who stand on each side does not refute the fact that these characters replace the more concrete characters of the fable. As a consequence, the conflict can now be easily won by the straight voice because it has a powerful set of allies against the rival voice.

At this juncture we see how our second problem becomes relevant, for the conflict between a crooked *logos* and a straight *logos* repeats the dichotomy inherent in the *logos* itself. As we have seen, Hesiod's view of the *logos* is characterized by contradictory elements. It may be an entity that imitates things with deflection and difference, and therefore would be false, crooked, and vicarious in relation to the things themselves. On the other hand, it speaks the truth, "sings the mind of unjust people,"[30] mirrors "things as they are," and goes directly to them.

We now see the *telos* of the impersonation of Hesiod's voice.[31] In the last scene, Dikê (straight judgment and Justice) is opposed to Hybris (crooked judgment and violence). Hybris, inasmuch as it is one with the crooked *logos* and the verdicts of the basileis, is then akin to the language of falsehood, violence, and forgetfulness. Dikê, on the contrary, with her straight judgments, is related to the attributes of the language of truth.

Though the religious characters who act in this conflict are not the same as those who represent the opposition between false and true discourse, they nevertheless have some common attributes. Dikê, for instance, is daughter of Zeus, as are the Muses, and both Dikê and the Muses enjoy the exclusive privilege of access to the original source; i.e., the Memory-Knowledge of "things as they are," and the straightening power of Zeus.[32]

However, the analogy that we are suggesting derives essentially from the reduction of the conflict between Dikê and Hybris to a conflict of *logoi*. The physical and bloody encounter between violence and justice that is represented in the encounter of the hawk and nightingale is replaced by a conflict of *logoi*. Just as Hybris has no more power than Dikê, so the arrogance and violence of the basileis have no greater power than the *voice* of the poet. On the contrary, endowed with divine favor, the poet's voice can overcome Hybris. The poet's voice is the straight one, identical to the truth that the Muses inspire in him; his voice mirrors the power, the presence, and the stability of Zeus, who straightens that which is crooked. By attributing the conflicting qualities of language to two opposing entities, the text frees Hesiod's *logos* of its dangerous aspects and guarantees it the divine power to be "straight," to mirror the truth. By placing Dikê[33] at the knees of Zeus, singing of the evils of unjust people, Hesiod in fact conveys his own desire to be heard by Zeus (*Erga* 5 ff.):

Easily he makes strong, easily he oppresses the
strong man, easily he humbles the proud and
raises the obscure, and easily he straightens the
crooked and bends the proud: Zeus, who thunders aloft
and dwells most high. Listen to me with eye and ear
and straighten the judgments according to justice,
and I will say, I think, the truth to Perses.

Hesiod's presentation of Dikê and the imperative prayer to Zeus in the
proemium involve the same gesture; the difference between the two is that
through the figure of Dikê, the *logos* acquires the force of a presence.

As I said in the beginning of this chapter, Hesiod succeeds in transforming
the lament of the nightingale into the voice of the goddess Dikê through a
series of figures: the image of the road, the personification of dikê, and the
belief in her divine ascendancy. In this way he has transformed the random
flight of the nightingale carried away by the hawk into a flight to the throne
of Zeus; he has introduced a safe space between the place where Dikê is still
insulted (*Erga* 258) and the place in which she responds to offence; he has
connected her voice to the paternal power and to his concern for justice. Consequently Hesiod has tried to write off whatever is random, senseless, and
deadly in the nightingale's lament—and in his own discourse. He has tried to
remove the difference of language and its relationship to death.

Yet this overall transformation of the nightingale's lament has failed to
transform language itself: the metaphors and the personification do not
transgress the limits of language, do not transform language into something
akin to the "original" locus of power. Hesiod still sings like the nightingale
pierced by the claws of the hawk. In the intention of the text Dikê should
derive force and power from her father; her words should mirror his consideration for justice: in the same way that the discourse of the Muses is
truthful because the goddesses are present where events occur, so the discourse of Dikê should be powerful because it mirrors the same concern that
the powerful father has. But this intention, this project, is frustrated to the
extent that the father is distracted: the voice of Dikê cannot itself become the
locus of original power and truth, and it remains vicarious and supplementary—
an addition to that *locus*. The text confirms the impossibility of this project in
several ways. The alternating impotence and strength that have characterized
Dikê's previous incarnations have already suggested the tensions between which
the voice of the poet oscillates. Moreover, as the voice of the poet identifies
itself with that of Dikê and obtains access to Zeus, the source of power, a
series of ambiguous reversals and incongruities follows. First, the basileis, though
they are lords of the city and "descendants of Zeus," are deprived of Zeus's pro-

tection and reduced to powerlessness. Second, the text exposes the *logos'* vicarious function in the figure of Dikê. Her visit to Zeus recalls similar scenes in epic, such as the one in which the wounded Aphrodite rushes to complain to her father, Zeus, only to receive a paternal warning to look after her own business and not to mingle in others'! But more significantly, Dikê's unveiling of "the mind of unjust people" is a totally superfluous action: Zeus's eye alone "sees everything, understands everything, and sees also these things, if he wants." Not only does Father Zeus not need his daughter's information—Dikê cannot even be assured that Zeus will be willing to see and to take into account that which she presents to him. The voice of Hesiod has become that of a goddess, a presence, and a power, yet it is still the same, desperate prayer of the *proemium*: though in the presence of Zeus, Hesiod's voice still responds to the ferocious claws of the hawk.

Since antiquity the surprising text of lines 267-73 has been considered spurious. Following the scholiast, Plutarch excised the passage because he could not accept the moral relativism it contained. Modern scholars accept the passage as genuine, but their explanations of its obvious inconsistency vary. Ehrenberg, p. 69, notices that though Dikê is a goddess, she does not act: "she is without any power; as she represents the rights of the weak, she is herself weak. . . . The goddess has received her first shape from the speculative imagination of the poet." In a note, Ehrenberg then explains the contradiction between the two portraits of Dikê by assuming that Hesiod created the second at a later writing. This sort of approach merely tries to justify the poet's inconsistency rather than explain it. Solmsen discusses the inconsistency, but he deems that it is only verbal:

> Finally, in the lines which may be regarded as the
> climax of the whole section, the poet assures us
> that Zeus' own eye sees everything and notices
> everything, so that there might seem to be little
> need for reporters and representatives on earth.
> The quick change from one religious image or
> proposition to the next shows unmistakably that
> each of them possesses for Hesiod symbolic, not
> literal, truth. The images vary, but each of them
> is merely the temporary external appearance of the
> idea, the body, so to speak, which the idea needs
> in order to become communicable. There may be
> inconsistency of verbal expression, but there is
> no inconsistency at all on the level of the idea
> itself, and the only inference which we may draw
> from the plurality and diversity of the religious

images which Hesiod here employs is that his
religious conviction is intense.

(p. 94)

But a faith in the divine Justice that controls the world coincides, in Hesiod's
text, with the acknowledgment of the powerlessness of Dikê. This is not a
simple verbal inconsistency. If Zeus were really present, neither Hesiod nor
Dikê would need to speak. But Hesiod's *logos*—and its metaphysical embodiment, Dikê—replaces the absent Zeus.

Indeed, the text strives to have both Zeus and Dikê present and identical
in lineage and power—father and daughter. Since Dikê embodies Hesiod's
voice, the text presents the image of a family relationship in which Hesiod's
voice plays the role of a son of Zeus. The boldness of this image elicits a tone
that is at once stupendously elated and arrogant. The daughter finally sings the
truth to the powerful father and commands his attention, but the text, in representing such a gesture, also suggests the distraction or even the absence of the
father's watchful eye. Thus the voice of the poet elicits the presence of the
father, but it simultaneously seems to replace that presence and, therefore,
displace it. The impatient son (Hesiod's voice, embodied in the figure of Dikê)
desires to assume the attitude and the power of the father; but any success the
son has in achieving this will dethrone the father.

In reality, however, Hesiod's voice merely replaces an absence: for if Zeus is
present, Dikê (i.e., Hesiod's *logos*) is unnecessary, and if Zeus is not present,
Dikê has no one whom she can address. This means that the father, the *locus*
of power and justice (like the *locus* of truth for the discourse of the Muses)
is always the figure that the *logos* assumes, as it tries to repress its own random
movements, vicariousness and difference. The father-and-son relationship is inscribed in the *logos* as a figure of its metaphysical aim.

The tremendous tension between the presence of Zeus and his absence, his
watchful eye and his distraction, explodes a few lines later when the poet, dis-
heartened by the sight of human affairs, bursts into expressions of despondency
and hope; he first rejects Justice as harmful in a world of injustice, but immediately afterward hopes for Zeus's protection of justice. As before, the split between despondency and faith suspends the text in an overall vibration. Hesiod's
coherence is finally demonstrated by the fact that the inconsistency is another
repetition of the pattern that controls all his work. The first paradox we discussed was "the deviating power of the straight *logos*"; this last inconsistency,
"the powerlessness of the goddess Dikê" merely repeats the pattern of that
paradox.

The most frequently cited books in this and the next chapter are the following:

Bona Quaglia, L. *Gli "Erga" di Esiodo*. Turin, 1973. (Hereafter cited as Bona Quaglia.)

Hays, H. M. *Notes on the "Works and Days" of Hesiod*. Chicago, 1918. (Hereafter cited as Hays.)

Puelma, M. "Sänger und König. Zum Verständnis von Hesiods Tierfabel." *Museum Helveticum* 29 (1972): 86–109. (Hereafter cited as Puelma.)

Sinclair, T. A. *Hesiod's "Works and Days"*. London, 1932. (Hereafter cited as Sinclair.)

Solmsen, F. *Hesiod and Aeschylus*. Ithaca, N.Y., 1949. (Hereafter cited as Solmsen.)

Troxler, H. *Sprache und Wortschatz Hesiods*. Zurich, 1964. (Hereafter cited as Troxler.)

Wilamowitz-Moellendorff, U. von. *Hesiodos Erga*. Originally published in 1928. Dublin/Zurich, 1970. (Hereafter cited as Wilamowitz.)

NOTES

1.   Ehrenberg, p. 69 maintains that in *Il*. 16. 387, dikê is personified and divinized. But he assumes that the passage is interpolated after Hesiod's *Erga* 221–24. I think that the Iliadic passage is genuine (see p. 67 ff. and note 21). Dikê, in the Iliadic passage, should probably be interpreted as a divine figure; abstract notions that are animated, as in this passage, become more or less daimonic in Homer. See Wilamowitz, p. 66.

2.   I agree with J. P. Vernant ("Le mythe hésiodique des races. Essai d'analyse structurale," *Revue d'histoire des religions* 157 [1960] : 21–56) that from 180 on Hesiod describes a new age, which is a deteriorated repetition of the present iron age. See also my paper, "Lévi-Strauss and the Classical Culture," *Arethusa* 4 (1971): 103 ff. J. Fontenrose ("Work, Justice, and Hesiod's Five Ages," *Classical Philology* 69 (1974): 1 ff.), while critical of Vernant's attempt to fit Hesiod's five ages into Dumézil's tripartite structure of Indo-European society, agrees with Vernant's view that Hesiod's five ages are synchronic as well as diachronic: "the myth is a paradigm, an *exemplum* of his argument, a synchronic scheme presented as history."

For an emphasis on the myth as an historical representation, see T. G. Rosenmeyer, "Hesiod and Historiography," *Hermes* 85 (1957): 257 ff.

3.   On the fable, see Puelma. The author presents a lucid and detailed analysis by which he convincingly confutes the arguments of those scholars who, until recently, denied any autobiographical reference in the fable. I agree fully with his interpretation that the fable sets up the confrontation between the poet and the basileis; i.e., between the spiritual, musical power of the singer and the worldly power of the kings (p. 92).

On αἶνος as a technical expression to designate a tale of beasts and plants see Puelma, p. 86, n. 2. Yet in Homer the word never has this meaning: it designates "des récits ou des propos édifiants, significatifs" (P. Chantraine, *Homère Iliade Chant XXIII* [Paris, 1964], p. 94).

In particular, αἶνος designates a discourse that aims at praising and honoring someone or something or at being ingratiating toward a person. Accidental or not, in Homer the word always defines a polite, edifying speech that is in direct or indirect connection with a gift or a prize. In *Il.* 23. 795 αἶνος means "praise," as is made evident by the verb κυδαίνω ("to give honor") of line 793. Achilles repays this αἶνος with a gift. In the same book, Nestor's speech—in which he recalls his past deeds and thanks Achilles for his generous gift—is termed an αἶνος (*Il.* 23. 652). In both poems we find πολύαινος as an epithet for Odysseus: in at least one passage the word is connected with Odysseus's cunning (*Il.* 11. 430), and in *Od.* 14. 508-9 Odysseus's speech—termed αἶνος—is explicitly defined as a discourse that will not "miss a reward." In *Od.* 21. 110 Telemachos turns to the suitors, who are ready to compete for Penelope's hand, and says rhetorically that she does not need any praise (αἶνος). Yet Telemachos has in fact praised Penelope and enhanced her unique qualities (106-9): he therefore increases the suitors' willingness to compete for the prize, i.e., for Penelope. In view of all of this, it is tempting to assume that Hesiod is purposely ambiguous in using the word αἶνος. The phrase "I'll tell an αἶνος to the basileis, wise men that they are" (*Erga* 202) might suggest a celebrative intention; the fable itself, concentrating on the hawk's speech, may appear, allegorically, as the justification and celebration of the kings' right and as a censure of the nightingale's foolishness. Yet the phrase is fraught with ambiguity. While in Homer the αἶνος is the polite, ingratiating, and edifying speech giving thanks for a received gift, in anticipation of a gift, or about a prize, here, by contrast, the αἶνος should remind us of the kings "who devour gifts." Moreover, the expression φρονέουσι καὶ αὐτοῖς may imply either Hesiod's polite apology ("even if the basileis, wise men that they are, do not need my αἶνος") or Hesiod's censure ("wise men though they be, this αἶνος [fable] will teach them a lesson"). See the commentaries by Hays, pp. 105-6), Sinclair, p. 25, and Bona Quaglia, p. 134.

4.   The diction of the fable shows great artistry. Hesiod echoes traditional formulas, reshapes them in order to establish the desired context (i.e., an allu-

sion that will have a bearing on his new content), and creates new phrases and puns.

To limit myself to some striking features: notice the pun ἀηδόνα: ἀοιδόν (see also n. 5) and the allusion to Homeric phrases that refer to the fight of heroes or gods. For instance, in *Il*. 21. 494 an ἴρηξ attacks a πέλεια, and in *Il*. 22. 139 ff. a κίρκος attacks a πέλεια. Both passages are similes referring to fighters. Analogously, the theme of the powerful one (κρείσσων) mocking the weaker who is vainly trying to resist (210-11) is even linguistically close to epic passages referring to fighters (see Puelma, pp. 89 ff and p. 93, n. 32). In this way the allegorical quality of the fable is made clear, and we are invited to see in the encounter between the hawk and the nightingale a heroic, though paradoxical, fight.

New phrases are: φρονέουσι καὶ αὐτοῖς | (202) (the closest Homeric correspondent is νοέοντι καὶ αὐτῷ | in *Il*. 23. 305 [see Hay's commentary]); ἀηδόνα ποικιλόδειρον (203); φέρων ὀνύχεσσι μεμαρπώς (204), which is a metrical equivalent of φέρων ὀνύχεσσι πέλωρον in *Il*. 12. 202, 220 and in *Od*. 15. 161, but which is syntactically transformed by the addition of μεμαρπώς, itself a participial form unprecedented in Homer; and δεῖπνον . . . ποιήσομαι, which is new both in its verbal connection and in the idea of "making a meal of somebody."

On line 207 see Puelma, p. 93, n. 33; on εἷς (208) see G. P. Edwards, *The Language of Hesiod in Its Traditional Context* (Oxford, 1971), p. 144.

Merkelbach proposed to read πρός τ᾽ ἄλγεσιν αἴσχεα (211) ("and suffers scorn besides pain") in order to respect the normal conceptual sequence expected in the proverb. See Puelma, p. 89, n. 15.

5.   In the use of ἀοιδός, Hesiod does not follow Homer: he never employs the Homeric formula θεῖος ἀοιδός (which occurs twelve times in Homer: eleven times closing the verse and once placed after the first foot of the verse); nor does he use any of the other Homeric epithets: πολύφημος, θέσπις ἐρίηρος. Yet he introduces the phrase ἀοιδὸς | Μουσάων θεράπων (*Th*. 99) so descriptive of his view of poetic inspiration.

On the pun ἀηδόνα : ἀοιδόν see Bona Quaglia, p. 132. The traditional etymology of both words, ἀειδεῖν, has been recently disputed. See H. Frisk *Griechisches etymologisches Wörterbuch* (Heidelberg, 1960); A. Pagliaro, "Aedi e rapsodi" in *Saggi di critica semantica* (Messina and Florence, 1953) p. 5, n. 3; and P. Chantraine, *Dict. étym.*

The epithet ποικιλόδειρος attributed to the ἀηδών (203) means literally "with a dappled neck": but it could also allude to the musical tones from the throat of the nightingale and the poet. Wilamowitz's note, p. 64, has his customary confidence: "Hesiod has put down ποικιλόδειρον without thinking

that the epithet does not befit a nightingale. The Byzantines have vainly
looked in it for πολύφωνον." But see δέρη as "throat" emitting sounds in
Aesch. *Ag.* 329. See also Puelma, p. 90, n. 22.

The mention of the hawk's readiness to devour the nightingale should recall the greedy hunger of the basileis, "devourers of gifts" (*Erga* 39, 221, 266).

6.   The etymology of ἀντιφερίζω is disputed (see *Lexikon des Früh. Epos*):
it is seen either as derived from ἀντιφέρομαι (Chantraine, *Gram. Hom.* 1: 340)
or as a derivation from ·φαρής(ἀντιφαρές· ἐναντίον [Hesych.] ; see Schwyzer,
Griechische Grammatik (Munich, 1939), p. 736, n. 5).

But the meaning of the verb in this passage of the *Erga* is clear: the verb
not only implies "to measure oneself with, " as it is used in the *Iliad* among
fighting gods and heroes (21. 357, etc., and see Puelma, p. 89, n. 16); more
precisely it often means "to fight" as it is shown by the word νίκης (*Lexikon
des Früh. Epos*, ibid.). On the ἰσηγορία of the nightingale see Puelma, pp. 100 ff.

7.   On ἐλεόν (*Erga* 205) see Troxler, pp. 172 ff. For "the glory of gods and
heroes" (κλεῖα or ἔργα ἀνδρῶν, θεῶν) see *Il.* 9. 189; *Od.* 1. 338, etc.

8.   Ἀκούω in the sense of "harken to," "obey," with inanimate nouns is
almost invariably followed by words meaning "discourse," "voice," or "cry,"
such as μῦθοι, βοή, etc. In the *Lexikon des Früh. Epos* (p. 431, section A IV 2),
Erga 213 (ἄκουε δίκης) is the only exception to that rule.

Becker, p. 87, capitalizes Ὕβρις at 214 and Ὕβριν and Δίκην at 217. I do
not understand why he does not do so at 213.

9.   See *Il.* 3. 62: ὀφέλλει δ' ἀνδρὸς ἐρωήν, etc.

10.   See Wilamowitz, p. 65.

11.   See Nicolai, pp. 53 ff. It is, furthermore, worth noting that the address to
Perses "deturns" the discourse from the basileis: Hesiod addresses him privately,
as if he does not expect the basileis to believe him.

12.   Hybris is also bad for weak people because, as Hesiod teaches (*Erga* 260-61),
the common people pay for the crimes of the basileis. For further discussion,
see Nicolai, p. 55 and n. 90.

13.   See *Erga* 216: ὁδὸς δ' ἑτέρηφι παρελθεῖν / κρείσσων ἐς τὰ δίκαια: literally
"The way on the other side to go to justice, is better." On ἑτέρηφι, see Troxler,
pp. 71 ff. Notice that κρείσσων picks up κρείσσονας of line 210; this directly
confutes the moral of the hawk.

14.   Cf. *Erga* 216 ff.: ὁδὸς δ' ἑτέρηφι κτλ.

In *Il.* 16. 734, and 18. 49 ἑτέρηφι is in opposition to the left. On *right* and
left in Homer, Hesiod, and Greek philosophy in general, see G. E. R. Lloyd,
"Right and Left in Greek Philosophy," *JHS* 82 (1962): 58 ff. and his *Polarity
and Analogy*, 1966, pp. 41 ff.

15.   On the cut between 218 and 219, see Nicolai, p. 57.

16. ἡ δ᾽ ἕπεται κλείουσα πόλιν καὶ ἤθεα λαῶν. The interpretations vary between: (1) Dikê, weeping, follows in the city and in the quarters of the people, etc. (Becker, p. 180; see also Hays, p. 109); (2) Dikê follows (where men drag her), weeping for the city and the quarters of people (Sinclair, p. 27; Colonna, p. 73). The former interpretation runs into difficulty with ἕπεται plus the accusative, which is not used in epic poetry. In the latter interpretation, one has to decide between two meanings of ἤθεα, both well illustrated in Hesiod: "abodes," "haunts," "quarters" or "customs"/"habits" (see Troxler, p. 168). In this passage both meanings are possible. As concerns κλαίω plus the accusative, see Il. 20. 210 and Od. 1. 363, where the verbs mean "to weep for someone" or "to mourn." This sense can be accommodated by our text. Though it seems shocking that Dikê should weep for the city while planning punishment for its citizens, this meaning can be supported. In fact, πόλις and λαοί mean the *people* in contrast to the basileis (or the crooked men), and evil is here planned by Dikê against the same basileis (224). Dikê might well be said to weep for the people, since they suffer both from the basileis's unjust verdicts and from the retribution that Zeus sends (238 ff. and, especially, 260–61).

17. To add to the other difficulties, Δίκης . . . ἑλκομένης can be taken either as a genitive absolute or as a genitive dependent on ῥόθος: i.e., "there is the lament of Dikê dragged. . . ."

18. The hawk can decide to eat the nightingale (209), and the basileis are defined as gift-eaters (δωροφάγοι [221]). This gluttony of the basileis, who are characterized as "swallowing" money or gifts, is comparable to the gluttony characteristic of the devil in other cultures.

19. In the passage we are analyzing, the doublet Dikê : δίκη (Justice : Verdict) appears often: Dikê-Justice, 220; σκολιαὶ δίκαι 221; μιν (i.e., Δίκην) : ἰθεῖαν (i.e., δίκην), 224; δίκας : δικαίους, 225 ff., etc.

20. Becker, p. 180, n. 73.

21. As a consequence of these movements of Dikê and Horkos, the image of the road, suggested in the Homeric text only by ἐκ [. . .] ἐλάσωσι, is enlarged in Hesiod, evoking also the city and the quarters (?) of men. On this line of interpretation see Gagarin, "Dikê in the *Works and Days*," p. 92.

There are other elements that point to Hesiod's dependence on Homer: the unexpected ἄνδρες (220) and ἄνθρωποι (223)—instead of basileis—picks up ἄνδρεσσι of Il. 16. 386. The rage of Zeus in the Iliad's text is maintained by Hesiod, but the daimonic participation is enlarged (see 249 ff.). In the Homeric text, Zeus's fury provokes natural violence—storm, flooding, and ravaged fields—but in Hesiod the manifestation of Zeus's fury takes on a more ethical form and strikes out at the society of men in the *polis*.

On the problem of the relationships between Homer and Hesiod in this passage, see Wilamowitz, p. 66, who describes the impression made on Hesiod by Homer's passage; Solmsen, p. 94, n. 79; Ehrenberg, p. 69; Krafft, pp. 78 ff., etc. Krafft, in particular, makes an interesting point about the difference between *dikai* and *themistai* in Hesiod.

22.   Compare especially 116 and 236: ἐσθλὰ δὲ πάντα τοῖσιν ἔην and θάλλουσιν δ'ἀγαθοῖσι διαμπερές. In the golden age, as in the City of Justice, only good exists forever. See also chapter 4, pp. 106 ff.

23.   I agree with Nicolai's opinion (p. 56) that this dikê refers to line 239 and means Zeus's "retribution." But others understand it in different ways: see Wilamowitz (p. 70, "meinen Rechtshandel," etc.); Nicolai, pp. 60 ff., n. 101; Quaglia, p. 137, n. 25. At 269 this justice (τήνδε δίκην) and τάδε (at 268) refer to the status of justice in Hesiod's city and therefore to Hesiod's personal case as well. (See Wilamowitz, p. 72; Sinclair, p. 31; but for other interpretations, see Nicolai, pp. 60 ff., n. 101.)

24.   Ὄπις may be translated as "eyes," "visitation," "anger," or "vengeance."

25.   The Greek is Δίκης Διὸς ἐκγεγαυῖα. There is no doubt in my mind that Hesiod wants to show how the name Dikê is formed from Διός. For Hesiod's taste for etymological jokes, puns, etc., see Troxler, pp. 8 ff.

26.   In Homer βλάπτω means "to stop the march," or to "bar the road" of a man, a horse, etc.; with a complement like φρένας it means "lead astray." Hence Sinclair translates it as "obstruct" or "debar", and the image of the road appears again. Yet *Erga* 365 contains βλαβερόν in the sense of "ruinous"; and here (258) it is difficult to see how Dikê could be obstructed in her march by crooked insults. It is easier to understand βλάπτω as "offend," "hurt," etc. As Solmsen notes (p. 92): "If Justice is a goddess, anyone who commits an injustice, especially one who delivers a crooked verdict in a lawsuit, offends a deity. . . ."

27.   There is an alternative to my translation: "It is right for a man to be bad when a more unjust man obtains greater justice."

28.   See Solmsen, p. 92, for confirmation of this.

29.   For the discussion on this ethical principle, see Quaglia, p. 139.

30.   The verb γηρύετ(ο) (260) is the same verb used to describe the Muses when they sing of truth in *Th.* 28.

31.   Dikê remains, through all the transformation she undergoes, essentially a voice. As a nightingale, she lamented; as a daimon on her road, she spoke ("Perses, harken to Dikê" [213]); as a captive woman, she wept; and as a daughter sitting near Zeus, she sang the mind of unjust people. This is no surprise, since Dikê in all her personifications exists only through a voice, that of the poet.

32.   One might add to this analogy that the obtuse shepherds—unable to understand the truthful voice of the Muses—and the violent basileis are both described by base images: "mere bellies" and "devourers of gifts," respectively.

33.   The epithet of Dikê, κυδρή, is used only for Hera (*Th.* 328) and Hecate (*Th.* 442). As Ehrenberg notes: "Dike ist jetz unter den Olympiern, da der Dichter betont (denn seine Hörer wissen davon bisher nichts) wie geehrt sie dort ist" (p. 69). Cf. Solmsen: "To practice justice, to recognize Dikê as the great goddess that she is (is she not much more important than Hera, Poseidon and Athena?) is the one thing that sets man apart from the animals and gives him his specific status and dignity" (p. 96).

Chapter 4

PANDORA

... from one link of a semeiotic nature (hence
also of a material nature) we proceed uninterruptedly
to another link of exactly the same nature. And
nowhere is there a break in the chain, nowhere
does the chain plunge into inner being, nonmaterial
in nature and unembodied in signs.

V. N. Vološinov

THE WORLD BEFORE PANDORA

Pandora is the last gift of the gods that I wish to discuss in the present context. The woman is a gift of Zeus to mortals, all of whom, until that moment,
had been male and had led a nearly godlike life. This is the common background
of both the *Theogony* and the *Erga*, in which the creation of Pandora occurs as
the last act of a series of incidents that lead mankind from its "natural" godlike
life to "culture" and the mortal life of toil. For this reason she is a *kakon*, a
bane to man. But how she constitutes such a bane, or what her precise crime
is, remains a complex question, to which there is no easy answer. It is, of course,
true that in the *Erga* she brings disaster by lifting the lid of the jar containing
thousands of evils, but this story does not appear in the *Theogony*. Moreover,
in both texts she is created with such attributes as to suggest a totally different
kakon in her person. When Zeus invents and defines her as "an evil gift in
which all men shall rejoice in their hearts, embracing their bane" (*Erga* 57–58),
he suggests a full range of flaws and vices inextricably connected with charm
and beauty: a set of paradoxical attributes hardly necessary for the task she
accomplishes in opening the jar. Pandora, in fact, lifts the lid of the jar consciously (ἐμήσατο [*Erga* 95]), but this gesture does not demand more than
a scheming mind. Finally, in both texts, Pandora is created by Zeus as a new
device and strategy in his fight against Prometheus. Prometheus, therefore, is

82

the real cause of the disaster that befalls mankind. However, the three acts of the whole episode—the quarrel between Zeus and Prometheus, the creation of Pandora,[1] and the story of the jar—do not seem to coalesce in a unified narrative as a coherent whole.[2] In fact, one wants to add various considerations, especially concerning the third episode, which is so loosely connected to the preceding one by only an adverb, "before," ($\pi\rho\iota\nu$ . . . [90 ff.]). Yet recent scholars (for instance, Krafft) have convincingly shown a consistent and meaningful unity of design. The unity of the episode has also been recently upheld by Vernant in an interpretation that sees Prometheus's and Pandora's stories as myths of origin. The myth of Prometheus is, for instance, at the base of various cultural traits in eating habits (the eating of meat), religious life (the establishment of sacrifice), and in technical experience (the discovery of a *techne* to produce fire). The myth of Pandora, in turn, establishes the heterosexual family for the purpose of reproduction, and the emergence of work and arts.

Many elements of this myth are common to myths of origin in other cultures. One has only to consult Frazer's *Myth of the Origin of Fire* and Lévi-Strauss's *The Raw and the Cooked* to confirm that fire, women, and mortality may often be connected in myths of origin and may be considered interchangeable, or analogous.

Consistent with the pattern of the myth of foundation, Hesiod's version represents Prometheus and Pandora as the points of origins of many factors in human life—*techne*, toil, sex, death—which did *not* exist before. In line with this intention, the myth calls for a polarized structure of terms in which nature is in opposition to *techne*, leisure to toil, natural reproduction to sex, and natural sleep to death.

This polarized structure should not surprise us; it is yet another *analogon* of what we have seen in Hesiod's language itself: the opposition of true to false, straight to crooked, etc. This structure, in the story of Prometheus and Pandora, allows the poet to pursue two arguments: to explain the beginning of culture, that is, the mode of life of present men; and to assess the value of this mode and suggest the possibility of a different way of life. For Hesiod, in fact, the "natural" mode of life constitutes the ideal one, and many of its important features appear in the idealized city governed with justice (*Erga* 227 ff.). The need for explanation and the edifying intention coincide.

Yet just as the text elsewhere does not consistently support the polarized structure of the terms qualifying language, here, too, a third element appears that overlaps and "precedes" the structure of contrasts; and analogously, this third element assumes the elusive form of an entity which *imitates* that which is true and original and, consequently, deflects from it (61–68). It is this particular quality of Pandora that interests us in her myth.

At the point at which the story begins in the *Erga*, Hesiod has been warning his brother—and, indirectly, the gift-devouring judges whom Perses trusts—that he must work himself, and not depend on the wealth of others. Zeus commands men to earn gifts from the earth through the appropriate work: "For (γὰρ [42]) the gods have hidden the livelihood of men, and keep it back." The narrative follows, quickly detailing the story of the quarrel between Zeus and Prometheus, which plays a larger part in the corresponding episode of the *Theogony*. But while in the *Theogony* the text gives precise "historical" detail about the moment of this quarrel, the text of the *Erga* is more elusive. In the *Theogony* (535-36) we learn that the beginning of the quarrel occurred at Mekone "when gods and mortal men departed," i.e., at their last common banquet. In the *Erga*, on the contrary, the existence of a paradisiacal community between gods and men is almost hidden in a conditional sentence that reads much like a wish: "[If Zeus had not hidden the means of livelihood]) you might lightly win even in one day sufficient food for you to live a whole year in leisure. Then you might put the rudder over the smoke, and the work of oxen and of patient mules would perish. But Zeus in his wrath, because . . . Prometheus had deceived him, concealed [the livelihood]"3 (*Erga* 43-46). Through this conditional sentence, our text evokes the golden age, of which we learn new details, this time in a sort of "historical" narrative, at 90 ff.:

> For indeed before [the coming of Pandora] men
> lived on the earth apart from (νόσφιν ἄτερ)4
> evil and apart from awful toil, and from cruel
> diseases that bring death to men.

The life described is reminiscent of the life men enjoyed at the time of the golden age (112 ff.):

> They lived like gods . . . apart from (νόσφιν
> ἄτερ) toils and woe. Neither were they
> subjected to miserable old age, but . . . they
> were apart from all evils. And they died as if
> overcome by sleep.

In order to stress the similarity between the two passages, I have quoted parts of lines 112-17; but, in addition to the absence of death, diseases, old age, toils, and woe,5 the text recalls other interesting themes. First is man's absolute "serenity of heart" (ἀκηδέα θυμὸν ἔχοντες [112]), a formula which repeats the perfect serenity of the Muses (*Th.* 61) and that of the heroes on the Isles of the Blessed (*Erga* 170). Pandora, on the contrary, devises κήδεα λυγρά (sorrows and griefs [95]). Second is the theme of man's *identity* with his original form throughout his life (αἰεὶ δὲ πόδας καὶ χεῖρας ὁμοῖοι [114]).

Man never aged, but remained identical to the form he took as he sprang from the Earth, for his descent was common to that of the gods (*Erga* 108–see nn. 13, 15).

With the appearance of woman, paradise ends. The quarrel between Zeus and Prometheus of course threatened man's happiness, especially because it provoked Zeus's wrath. But as long as Zeus and Prometheus continued to play their game of hiding and uncovering things, man would ultimately be none the poorer. In this cosmic "hide and seek" between the two gods, fire is first lost and then found again for men. Despite the fact that the new fire is no longer natural, and though Prometheus's scheming, deviousness,[6] and theft[7] make him a divine representative of Perses, the tone of the narration is pleasant. The text stresses Zeus's wisdom and familiarity with lightning at the very moment when Prometheus fools him:

> On his turn[8] . . . [Prometheus] stole fire for
> men from Zeus the wise in a hollow fennel stalk,
> escaping the notice of Zeus, who delights in lightning
> (50–52).

A NEW PORTENT: GLAMOR AND DIFFERENCE

Suddenly Zeus changes his strategy: instead of hiding something else from mortals, he decides to invent something new to send them, and now the trouble begins. The text marks the novelty of Zeus's strategy in several ways: angry until line 54, Zeus laughs after announcing his new weapon (59). Naive and duped as he has seemed until line 53, Zeus now finds a new tone, mocking the mocker (55 ff.); and, as he turns to the gods to order the creation of Pandora, he recommends the greatest urgency (ὅττι τάχιστα [60]). Indeed, a laborious manufacturing process begins: gone are the hiding and revealing, theft and furtiveness of the previous act (κρύψαντες [42], ἔκρυψε [47], κρύψε [50], ἔκλεψ' [51], λαθών [52]); we now witness the preparation of a gift, of a new being, of a supplement (δώσω κακόν [57], πλάσσεν [70], τεῦξε [79], Πανδώρην [81], δῶρον ἐδώρησαν [82] etc.). The molding of a new entity, the sending of a gift[9] to the perfect human society, destroys perfection. Zeus's token is at once a present, a destructive portent, and a lesson: it betokens man's fall.

The emphasis given by the text to the novelty of Pandora both as a new strategic maneuver on the part of Zeus (*adding* something instead of *hiding* something) and as an entity with *new, unprecedented* qualities (a mortal female) tends to obscure the formal parallelism that exists between Pandora and the previous exchange of gifts and hostile acts. Prometheus offers a deceptive dish at the banquet (*Th.* 538 ff.), and Zeus—cryptic as his reasons may sound—lets himself be deceived by it. Prometheus's ambiguous gift bears a formal similarity to Pandora: the appearance is appetizing, but the inner content is worthless. Similarly, Pandora is as beautiful as a goddess, but she has the deceiving mind of a shrew.

As a result of Prometheus's trick, Zeus cancels the gift of fire (οὐκ ἐδίδου [*Th.* 562] implies the previous gift of "natural" fire); Prometheus in turn provides man with "technical" fire, which can be considered a substitute for natural fire. The game, therefore, which unites Zeus, Prometheus, and man, consists of an exchange of gifts that implies a skillful substitution of that which is real, original, or good for that which is like the original only *in appearance*. Prometheus, then, is responsible for initiating the process of substitution of the imitation for the original.

Formally, therefore, Pandora as a gift of Zeus is analogous to the gifts exchanged earlier, but the text obscures this formal analogy. First, the text is vague about what Pandora replaces. Indeed, we understand that as she is added to the human scene, something else is subtracted from human society. As woman appears, livelihood and godlike life vanish. But the reader remains under the impression that she befalls man as a *new, unnecessary* being, as a replacement of nothing, as a total evil. Unlike fire, she seems to provide men only with burdens. Furthermore, she possesses an oxymoronic quality not inherent in the other gifts; for Pandora is pleasant and dangerous, an excess and a loss. She is an excess because she introduces toil as the way of producing what the earth once provided spontaneously, and a loss because toil does not fully restore the goodness of the preceding life.

Precisely because she is both excess and loss, she represents the beginning of an asymmetrical movement. For until her appearance, a sort of symmetry—however formal or simulated—existed: Zeus and Prometheus are both gods; each move of their quarrel constitutes a balanced action, hiding and uncovering. But when Pandora appears as an excess, the movement of asymmetry—and of history—begins.

The attributes of Pandora—addition to a perfect state of identity, and loss—qualify her as a "supplement" or, like Dikè, as a vicarious figure. The term "supplement" (which Derrida has elaborated with respect to language) implies a double movement: the supplement comes as an addition and, simultaneously, as a replacement. Language as "imitation" constitutes just this movement: it adds itself as a copy, as a repetition, and simultaneously replaces the "original." Since the original manifests itself only and always within and through the *logos*, it is inscribed in this very process of replacement. Analogously, Pandora emerges as imitation and as supplement.

As for lines 61–68, two importantly linked themes are to be stressed:
(1) Pandora as a novelty on the earthly scene, and (2) Pandora as an oxymoron
or a paradox, for, inasmuch as she is an *imitation* of that which already exists,
she cannot be entirely new.

As Zeus laughs, he turns to the gods (*Erga* 60–68):

> He ordered famous Hephaistos to mix earth
> with water immediately and to put therein man's language
> and strength and make this thing look like the
> immortal goddesses in the face, with the
> beautiful, lovely aspect of a virgin. Then
> he ordered Athena to teach her handiwork, to weave
> the embroidered web; and golden Aphrodite to shed
> around her head grace, grievous desire, and ruinous
> concerns. And Hermes, the messenger Argheiphontes,
> he bade give her shameless mind and cheating soul.

Before commenting on this passage line by line, let me point out that Zeus's
order is expressed in nine lines of indirect discourse. In the corresponding passage of the *Theogony* we have no specific order from Zeus, only the description
of Pandora's creation, "following the will of Zeus" ($K\rho o\nu i\delta\epsilon\omega$ $\delta\iota\grave{\alpha}$ $\beta o\nu\lambda\acute{\alpha}\varsigma$
[572]).

In the *Erga*, Zeus speaks in *direct* discourse to Prometheus (54–58),
mocking and threatening him; but the text *reports* his order commanding the
gods to manufacture Pandora. This prolonged development of indirect discourse is known to Homer, but it occurs rather rarely, for a long order is
habitually told in *oratio recta*,[10] and indirect discourse is more often contained in direct discourse.[11]

Besides this usual epic preference for direct discourse, we should also note
the modality of indirect discourse. By simply reporting the content of another's
utterance, indirect discourse tends to flatten the speech of the other by effacing
emotional and affective accents. In this way, indirect discourse achieves two
effects. On the one hand, it effaces the personality and presence of the speaker.
Here, for instance, it is not by chance that Zeus disappears behind Hesiod's
words: this relative and only incipient effacement corresponds to the elusive
presence and minimal effectiveness of Zeus in the remaining parts of the story.
During the actual manufacture of Pandora, for instance, the gods interpret
Zeus's order very freely, but the father of the gods does not seem concerned.
Yet he must be there, since he gives the order, again indirectly reported ($\pi\acute{\epsilon}\mu\pi\epsilon$
$\pi\alpha\tau\acute{\eta}\rho$ [84]), to deliver Pandora to Epimetheus. Similarly, in the scene of the
vase, Zeus's presence is explicitly reported only once (99). Since Zeus does

not seem to be present, however, scholars have considered this line an inter-
polation. The indirect discourse by which the poet reports Zeus's words corresponds, therefore, to his minimal presence. It seems as if Zeus, the inventor and
father of Pandora, is effaced or absorbed by Pandora at the very moment he is
"programming" her.

On the other hand, the effacement of the speaker's intentions, personal
accents, and exclamatory tones (see by contrast Zeus's utterance in 54–58)
enhances the factual, economic aspect of the message. Here, for instance, the
text can discount the formal expressions of address to the four gods, the verb
of volition for each god (an exception is line 68), and all emotional elements
outside the sense of urgency (ὅττι τάχιστα, "immediately").[12] Thus Pandora
constitutes the only content of the message, as Hesiod transmits it to us. Moreover, by delivering the message through the device of indirect discourse, Hesiod
takes upon himself the responsibility for the words of Zeus.

Zeus envisages the production of Pandora in six actions performed by four
different gods; these actions concern the manufacture of Pandora's body and
physical attributes. Zeus engages Hephaistos to mix Earth with water, to bestow force and voice/language, and to make Pandora look like the goddesses.
Three other actions concern the forming of Pandora's mind. Zeus engages
Athena to teach her arts, Aphrodite to give her loving and alluring attributes,
and Hermes to provide her with a treacherous mind.

This perfectly balanced division between physical and mental attributes (a
division probably new with Hesiod: see Krafft, pp. 48 ff.) produces a being
true to Zeus's oxymoron: beautiful in its outward aspect but pernicious inside.

> Line 61:
> γαῖαν ὕδει φύρειν
> (mix earth with water).

These words describe the substance of which Pandora is composed: earth and
water. She is molded like a vase by Hephaistos, and in the following lines Pandora is described as a container into which the gods put something (61 and 67).

The manufacture of the first woman (*Th.* 513–14, 588 ff.) debases and hu-
milates woman in comparison to man. According to one version (*Erga* 108, and
frg 1.6, Merkelbach-West, *Fragmenta Hesiodea* (Oxford, 1967), pp. 3 ff.), men and
gods emerged from the same place, presumably the earth, and, again presumably,
as whole beings.[13] According to another version, on the contrary, the gods
created (ἐποίησαν) men (*Erga* 109–10, 126–27, etc.). Philologists have applied
their acumen to softening the contradiction,[14] but without any persuasive results. Perhaps we should simply accept the two versions as contradictory, which

would imply that Hesiod juggles two different versions of man's creation and does not succeed in or does not care about resolving the inconsistency. We should realize that each version has its contextual coherence and that each presents the same theme: the decline of man from his original happy state. In fact, the two stories can be considered alternative (ἕτερον λόγον [*Erga* 106; see also chap. 4, n. 4]); they certainly depict the same line of development from a paradisiacal status to man's present and actual life.[15]

Though in line 61 there is no reference to the male's mode of birth, the audience already knows that man exists. As a first consequence, therefore, the woman appears to have been born late, marked off from man's lineage. Insofar as the text evokes the former happy community of men and gods (*Erga* 43 ff.; *Th.* 535 ff.), the woman is also marked off from man's origin, as he was born in the same place as the gods.

The diverse mode of emergence of the male and the female sets and seals an edifying and ideological principle; it polarizes male and female in antithetical terms. The opposition might suggest the later opposition of φύσις and τέχνη: the female as a product of arts would appear on the side of τέχνη rather than that of φύσις, which, on the contrary, produces males. This different mode of birth also introduces a distinction between what is originary—men and gods—and what comes later and, therefore, is no longer original. And finally, in this chain of contrasting terms, the female is not only an artificial product—just as is the πίθος whose lid she is going to lift—but also the bearer of arts and artifice.

The reader would certainly like to know what Hephaistos does with this molded piece of earth, whether he bakes it or animates it without any further manipulation. There is not a word in the text that would enlighten us on this point, and we can only speculate that he probably does bake it.[16]

Lines 61-62:

> ἐν δ' ἀνθρώπου θέμεν αὐδὴν
> καὶ σθένος, ἀθανάτης δὲ θεῆς εἰς ὦπα ἐίσκειν ...
> and to put therein man's language and strength and
> make this thing look like the immortal goddesses in
> the face. . . .

Pandora receives voice and language from man, but it is from the goddesses that she takes her beautiful face. Men and goddesses are the *models* from which she derives characteristics the same as, or similar to, theirs. Pandora, therefore, emerges as a copy, as an imitation of what already exists as original or archetypal. For Pandora will then become a pupil of Athena and will receive other traits from Aphrodite and Hermes, traits which are original with these gods. Her name, Pandora, as it is explained by Hesiod himself (81-82), implies that she is a gift from all the gods and, therefore, is a patch-work of various talents, traits, and qualifications preexisting her creation. Consequently, the first woman, the carrier of new evils, of arts and death, toil, sexuality, etc., derives these evils from their original possessors. She imi-tates the gods and the goddesses, in a human way, becoming similar and yet different from them. Thus, on the one hand, Pandora represents the term of a polarity in which she constitutes the beginning, or the origin, of various traits of the human race; on the other hand, she occupies this starting point *in medias res*, inasmuch as she *imitates* for the first time what exists as *original* before her.

Let us explore the expression ἐν δ' ἀνθρώπου θέμεν αὐδὴν καὶ σθένος. The phrase simply means "putting therein man's voice and strength," im-plying the ability to speak and the physical strength that men have today as they had before Pandora. But if one begins to question the emphasis of the text and to ask how this phrase pertains to the "natural" man before Pandora, all sorts of problems arise. Hesiod's expressions seem reminiscent of *Il.* 18. 419-20, in which Homer describes the golden handmaidens of Hephaistos: they are similar to living girls, possess mind, voice, and vital strength, and they have learned works from the gods: τῆς ἐν μὲν νόος ἐστὶ μετὰ φρεσίν, ἐν δὲ καὶ αὐδὴ / καὶ σθένος, ἀθανάτων δὲ θεῶν ἄπο ἔργα ἴσασιν. If Hesiod composed his text with the Homeric text in mind (Krafft, pp. 47-48), his deviations from Homer deserve our closest attention. Homer's text does not present the opposition so artfully worked out by Hesiod between man and gods: ἀνθρώπου . . . θεῆς. The golden maids in Homer possess unspecified language, force, and intelligence, and the poet stresses his amazement that mere statues possess the attributes of living beings. Though these attributes are probably of an immortal nature,[17] the Homeric text does not make this point. Had Hesiod simply wanted to say that Pandora is prodigiously alive, though manufactured in clay, he could simply have used the Homeric pat-tern. But he obviously wants to emphasize the human quality of that voice/ language,[18] as αὐδή by itself evokes the human voice.[19] If this emphasis on the human voice/language and strength of Pandora is seen in the context that affirms the novelty of her attributes, pitting a past status against a new one, we may draw conclusions from what is implicit in the text. Man, before Pan-dora, lived in community with the gods, without diseases, old age,[20] or death (*Erga* 92). Should not σθένος (force) suggest, then, the *vital force*[21] of present men? If it does, as the text seems to grant, then Pandora introduces for the first time among men the cycle of age, disease, and death. We know that she actually introduces these beginnings of human decay when she lifts the lid of the vase; it should not be surprising, then, that she carries them in her person. The myth would in this way guarantee that redundance that is typical of the genre. With this interpretation, Pandora appears as the carrier of man's difference and man's distance from the gods. Moreover, in this way, the textual emphasis on the contrast between human and godlike traits would find a motivation that is not just rhetorical.

The same argument should be applied to language: Pandora introduces the exclusivity of human language. She speaks only human language and, therefore is the first human who can no longer speak the language of the gods, of which Homer knows some words and to which Hesiod alludes in *Th.* 837.[22]

Although there is no evidence for claiming its necessity and absolute correctness, this interpretation of lines 61–62a is supported by the rhetorical emphasis of the text and by the logical tenets of the context.[23] The view that we propound, besides being consonant with the "novelty" of Pandora, uncovers and recovers the profound coherence of the text. For the manufacture of Pandora from a mixture of earth and water announces, in addition to her frailty and mortality, the shaping of heterogeneous elements in order to create a form. This *techne* of creation, by combining elements and by giving them a form resembling something else, cannot but evoke the *techne* of imitation *par excellence*, the articulation of sounds as language. Pandora represents the "figura" of this first imitation, of this excess that adds itself to that which is original, and she is coherently the "original" moment of human language.

> Lines 62–63:
> ... ἀθανάτης δὲ θεῆς εἰς ὦπα ἐίσκειν
> παρθενικῆς καλὸν εἶδος ἐπήρατον·
> ... and make this thing look like the immortal
> goddesses in the face, in relation to the beautiful,
> lovely aspect of a virgin ...

These lines are written in such a way as to weave together various elements reminiscent of the Homeric text. Line 420 of *Il.* 18: καὶ σθένος, ἀθανάτων δὲ θεῶν ἄπο ἔργα ἴσασιν, resonates in this passage along with another allusion to Homer (*Il.* 3. 158):

αἰνῶς ἀθανάτῃσι θεῇς εἰς ὦπα ἔοικεν
... she marvelously resembles the immortal goddesses
in her face . . .

This last line describes Helen in the admiring words of Priamos, the old king
of Troy. Yet another Homeric echo is present (*Od.* 6. 151-52):

'Αρτέμιδί σε ἐγώ γε · · ·
εἶδός τε μέγεθός τε φυήν τ'ἄγχιστα ἐΐσκω

These two lines constitute a conventional formula used to describe the beautification of a hero. As a result of this conflation of formulaic phrases the text
sounds, if not as though it had been put together piecemeal, at least redundant.
For whether we take εἶδος as the object of ἐΐσκειν ("to make her virgin's beautiful lovable aspect like the goddess in the face") or (see *Od.* 6. 151) we understand αὐτήν as the object of ἐΐσκειν ("to make her like the goddesses in the
face, in relation to the lovely, beautiful aspect of a virgin"), in both cases the
face is singled out as special in relationship to the body or the general appearance.

Pandora imitates the goddesses only partially, specifically in the face, and
therefore, as an imitation, she is unevenly or inconsistently modeled. Furthermore the outward beauty of Pandora—the only fully positive trait of the first
woman—is not without a foreboding quality. For the Homeric reminiscence
from the third book of the *Iliad* evokes the *first* Greek war and announces those
spiritual traits that connote Pandora's mind, which, like that of Helen, is the
mind of a bitch. With the advent of woman, war is at the gate.

Lines 63-64:
... αὐτὰρ 'Αθήνην
ἔργα διδασκῆσαι, πολυδαίδαλον ἱστὸν ὑφαίνειν

Then he ordered Athena to teach her handiwork,
to weave the embroidered web . . .

Having learned a skill from the gods, Pandora will introduce the arts into the
world, where men had previously lived in a state of leisure. The word ἔργα
recalls ἄεργον of line 44 and the whole passage of lines 43-44: until the
emergence of Pandora men did not *learn* and were not *taught*; with Pandora,
teaching—that is, the process by which a pupil imitates his master, and by
which an art is learned—emerges.

Curiously, the text does not enhance Athena with any personal epithet—
she is the only god in this passage so little honored—whereas it is repetitive
in mentioning her craft.[24] Of course, since weaving is a gift of Athena (*Od.*
7. 110), the epithet πολυδαίδαλον also characterizes Athena herself. This
epithet plays on a sort of assonance with διδασκῆσαι (popular etymology
connects the two words), and therefore it sheds some of its connotation onto
the pupil of Athena. Pandora—a product of divine skills—also imitates the
gods by learning the divine arts.

Lines 65-66:
καὶ χάριν ἀμφιχέαι κεφαλῇ χρυσῆν Ἀφροδίτην
καὶ πόθον ἀργαλέον καὶ γυιοκόρους μελεδώνας
and golden Aphrodite to shed grace around her head,
grievious desire and ruinous concerns . . .

The *charis* (grace) that Aphrodite is to bestow on Pandora introduces a
novelty in the world of man, since sexual pleasure from a woman, and
probably sexual pleasure itself, was unknown to man before Pandora's birth.
Zeus's portentous token elicits a new pleasure (τέρπνος), of which Zeus
speaks in his paradoxical statement about Pandora herself (57-58).[25] According to Zeus's intention, men will enjoy embracing their *kakon*; consequently, here the paradoxical intention is precisely fulfilled. Notwithstanding
the similarity between line 65 and the Homeric formula implying the extol-
ling and beautification of a hero (τῷ κατέχευε χάριν κεφαλῇ τε καὶ ὤμοις
[*Od.* 6. 235]), Aphrodite's *charis* is intended here *in malam partem* as well.
This *charis* must provoke an anguishing desire, ruin peace of mind, and create
fatiguing concern. The text is forcefully and skillfully elaborated: ἀργαλέον
recalls in sound and etymology the word ἄλγος; the expression γυιοκόρους
μελεδώνας[26] constitutes a double play on words, for γυιοκόρους means
"fatiguing, satiating the limbs"; and μελεδώνη was thought by the ancients
to be composed of μέλη and ἔδειν.[27]
    Line 66 admits of two possible interpretations. Wilamowitz had remarked
that πόθον (desire) and μελεδώνας (concern) are attached zeugmatically to
χάριν ἀμφιχέαι, "because they are not properly in the woman herself, but
she can receive only that which she will later arouse in men" (p. 49). The
zeugma, then, unites what she is (grace) and what she inspires in others
(desire and concern); the zeugma yokes the self and the other in a unity.
Pandora is at the origin of the opposition "self:other," but she still yokes
both terms in herself, for she is difference and the movement of difference.

However, there is no absolute need to assume the zeugma: the desire and concern could well be the attribute that the god assigns to Pandora along with grace. In fact, we see in the *Odyssey* that Penelope in love "melts with desire" (ἀλλ᾽ Ὀδυσῆ ποθέουσα φίλον κατατήκομαι ἦτορ [*Od.* 19. 136]) and suffers with deep concern (*Od.* 19. 516 f.):

> κεῖμαι ἐνὶ λέκτρῳ, πυκιναὶ δέ μοι ἀμφ᾽ ἀδινὸν κῆρ
> ὀξεῖαι μελεδῶναι ὀδυρομένην ἐρέθουσιν.
> I lie in bed, and sharp concerns, filling tight my
> heart, excite my crying.

If so, Pandora contains a split within herself: she makes the other a captive of her beauty, but she also becomes a captive of the other because of her desire and concern for him.

The text permits both interpretations: the latter because it is syntactically natural and the former because it responds more precisely to Zeus's paradoxical intention. However, in both cases Pandora introduces the division and the anguish for that division between the self and the other. As human language deviates and moves obliquely in its encounter with the other, it befits Pandora, the bearer of language, to seduce and fascinate the other and simultaneously to harm him (or herself). The fascination of Pandora's beauty, like the fascination of language, constitutes "glamor," true to its etymology (it is derived from "grammar"); for the spell of language and the spell that beauty casts upon the other are similar. Both inspire the torpor of oblivion, the effacement of the self and of the present, in the perspective of death. In fact, Pandora presents herself to Epimetheus, accompanied by Hermes (a Hermes, as we shall see, almost "Psychopompos"), and her beauty acts as a *dolos* (83), or trick. Epimetheus "*does not pay attention*" (οὐδ᾽ . . . ἐφράσαθ᾽) to what his brother had told him (85 ff.). Epimetheus *forgets* the warning and accepts Pandora; only when he already possesses the evil does he understand (89). Again, in this respect, Pandora acts as the fascination of language: her real nature can be understood by man only after he has accepted her.

In order to perfect the creation of Pandora, Hermes will add to her the mind of a "bitch" and a treacherous soul (67–68). This maleficent disposition makes her suitable for the task of destroying human happiness. Installed in Epimetheus's house and devising baneful plans for men, she will lift the lid of the vase.

Here Zeus's command ends: he lets the gods manufacture Pandora as he has ordered. In one reading of the story he seems almost to disappear from the human scene, leaving Pandora alone to work out man's destruction. But, as we shall see, he is not far away.

Zeus has conceived a being of the sort that will be needed for the task of destroying man's happiness, which will take place in the third episode. But Zeus has not merely hidden a tricky and deceiving mind under the glamorous face of Pandora: the glamor of Pandora hides the grin of death. Pandora appears as a novelty on the human scene because she is the bearer of language, violence, premature death, the arts, sexual pleasures, and treachery. If our interpretation is correct, she was, in fact, born with some of the qualities that she supposedly releases later by lifting the lid of the jar. In reality, the two narratives, the two acts of the episode—the creation of Pandora and the lifting of the lid of the jar—betoken the origin of death.

Pandora functions as the negative pole; the positive is the paradise that she replaces. This emphasis on her negative role obscures the important trait that we have forcefully elicited, the fact that Pandora is actually a copy, an imitation, of what existed before her. In this light we view Pandora as the "figura" (the rhetorical image and the personification) of difference and deferral, and as the coherent display of the two movements or functions of difference and deferral.

Pandora *replaces* what is original and true by a devious movement. Her function as "replacement" is explicitly stated by the poet, though the text does not make sufficiently clear *what* she replaces. In the *Erga* 57 (and with a slight variation in *Theogony* 570), we read

τοῖς δ' ἐγὼ ἀντὶ πυρὸς δώσω κακόν
To men, instead of fire I'll give an evil.

The expression ἀντὶ πυρός (in place of, instead of, fire) raises problems. In the compressed narrative of *Erga* and in the larger one of the *Theogony*, fire emblematizes the gift of Nature that Zeus decides to refuse to mortals (*Th.* 561 ff.; *Erga* 50). In this connection, the expression "in place of fire I'll give Pandora" can mean that Pandora will replace Nature's prodigious gift to man, that is, his Edenic status. Yet, since the refusal of fire signifies Zeus's intention to punish man, the same text can also mean: "Pandora is a punishment to "counterbalance the advantage that mankind acquired from stolen fire" (West, pp. 325–26). The first meaning describes Pandora as a replacement for paradise, and she is certainly that. She replaces it by imitating the attributes of both men and gods. Though the text does not elaborate further, we can supply the argument implicit in the intuition of the myth. Pandora takes the place of the "original" just as she imitates the absent "original"; the corruption that she introduces in the human scene derives from the process of displacements, deviations, and differences. Pandora epitomizes the process and accounts, therefore, for the corruption of paradise.

This brings me to the second point that I wish to elucidate. Pandora obviously establishes Hesiod's metaphysical separation of Nature and Culture by representing, in Hesiod's terms, the negativity of Culture; but, in truth, she is the "figura" of the movement that unites and comprehends the oppositions. For Pandora is what leads to the "same," through a movement of mimesis, displacement, and protraction. In this sense, she is the term contiguous to the oppositions, not a pole of the oppositions. In fact, she is prior to the opposition "Nature : Culture," since she comprehends the two poles: she looks like a Nature that has been *technically* restored and like a Culture that replaces Nature. Both terms are inscribed in her as supplement.

We shall return to this point after the analysis of the actual manufacture of Pandora by the gods.

THE BRIDE: A GIFT OF ZEUS

The gods, invited by Zeus to manufacture Pandora, respond with sufficient vagueness and independence to make the whole passage (68–82) suspect, in the opinion of many philologists. It is indeed difficult to define exactly what happens in the text; and, though words like "patchwork" and "inauthentic" are inappropriate and misleading, the critic should expose the divergence between Zeus's command and the manufacture of Pandora by the gods.

A basic consistency and coherence between the two passages can be detected, but it is within this coherence that the divergence acquires significance. In a certain sense, C. Robert[28] is correct in pointing out that the gods translate Zeus's orders into concrete terms. But something more precise than this happens. To begin with, the balanced tripartition that we have seen in Zeus's command (three actions concerning Pandora's physical attributes and three actions concerning her mind) is broken. The physical, material manufacture of Pandora requires only one action,[29] whereas her adornment takes four (if line 76 is genuine), and her mental equipment, two (lies and voice/language). The heavy emphasis placed on Pandora's ornaments intimates the specific novelty of this passage: what Zeus had conceived Pandora to be is given form in a personage full of *tokens* and *signs* of Zeus's original conception. In order to make this clear, we can first analyze the task that Zeus delegates to Aphrodite (73–75). First of all, Aphrodite does not appear, but sends in her place some of her occasional helpers to beautify Pandora. The goddess is, then, *vicariously* represented by the Charites, Peitho, and the Horai, all of whom may bespeak her, but none of whom is a univocal "sign" of Aphrodite.

Secondly, the *charis* (grace) that Aphrodite is to bestow upon the woman is replaced by golden necklaces. This replacement occurs smoothly; first, because the Charites (73) who adorn Pandora are somehow the impersonation of Aphrodite's *charis* (65); secondly, because the epithet of Aphrodite, "golden," is attributed to the necklaces (ὅρμοι). The text suggests, therefore, that some of Aphrodite's *charis* does pass to Pandora.[30] But in this way the actual grace of Aphrodite, with its ominous power, is represented by a vicarious image, a metonymic token of it: the golden necklaces.

The powerful evocation of desire and painful cares, the common territory unifying the self and the other, is replaced by the image of Pandora dressed for wooing or wedding. The Horai, in fact, crown Pandora with spring flowers (75), ornaments that announce a festive, religious occasion. (In the *Theogony* 576-78, if we assume the text is sound,[31] the woman gets both a crown and a golden *stephane*, an ornament hitherto belonging exclusively to goddesses and old heroines.)[32] In Hesiod's work, floral wreaths appear for the first time in Greek literature.[33] Their "novelty" stresses not only the novelty of Pandora in the world, but also the special nature of the occasion that calls for this kind of adornment.[34]

All these figurative elements about Pandora, these *tokens* and *signs* of Aphrodite and of her helpers,[35] reduce Pandora's original ominous power. She emerges tamed and faded, no longer a Helen or a Clytemnestra, but a "modest" (71) and beautiful girl, ready for her wedding in the colorful season of spring, distant and removed from the awesome presence of Aphrodite, of whom she carries only the signs.

It is fully consistent with this expansion of her symbolic attributes that the woman receives a symbolic name, "Pandora."[36] Zeus had left her nameless, but Hermes, at the end of the creation, bestows on her a very "significant" name:

$$\text{ὀνόμηνε δὲ τήνδε γυναῖκα}$$
$$\text{Πανδώρην, ὅτι πάντες 'Ολύμπια δώματ' ἔχοντες}$$
$$\text{δῶρον ἐδώρησαν, πῆμ' ἀνδράσιν ἀλφηστῆσιν.}$$

(*Erga* 80-82)

and [Hermes] named this woman Pandora, because all those
who live in the house of Olympos gave her as a
gift, a bane to men who eat bread.

This etymological explanation results in an amusing play on words. First of all, Hesiod disregards the other meaning of "Pandora" ("she who has [brings] all gifts)[37] and interprets the name as "a gift to men given by all gods." This interpretation is consistent with the thrust of the scenes we have just read: Zeus's intention of sending an evil gift to men and the role of the gods in the manufacture of that gift. Pandora therefore is a gift-bane (line 82) to man and a gift ($\delta\tilde{\omega}\rho o\nu$ [85, 86]) to Epimetheus.

On the other hand, in antiquity (see the discussion in C. Robert, p. 25) the text ὅτι πάντες . . . δῶρον ἐδώρησαν was already being interpreted to mean "because all the gods had given her a gift." This interpretation is formally correct and is justified by a certain context, for indeed many gods, as we have seen, do give her gifts, and Pandora is intended as an evil for man.[38]

The conclusion to which some scholars are forced is that here, as in many other passages of Hesiod, the text is purposely ambiguous, and both interpretations are possible. But if we keep in mind the three meanings of the word "Pandora," in so doing we shall understand the playfulness and irony of the etymology: Pandora, the all-giving, is instead a gift-bane to man, and (or because) she takes gifts from everybody. The mocking purpose and the edifying thrust of this joke is obvious, but a more serious implication is discernible when the pun is analyzed in the light of the ambiguities that mark the *gifts* of the gods.

The gift of the gods (see my introduction) is often paradoxical on two accounts: (1) though a gift, it cannot be rejected; (2) it implies some tricky, unresolvable quality. When we take into consideration the characteristics of the divine gifts, the reason that Hesiod effaces one legitimate meaning of Pandora ("she who has, or brings all gifts") in favor of the meaning supported and explained by the story of her creation becomes understandable. Hesiod in this way defines her both as being in a category of unwanted and inevitable gifts and as a paradoxical, deceptive trap that is impossible for men to avoid—a "gift-bane," as he says (*Erga* 82).

At the same time, we should keep in mind the other legitimate and obvious meaning of Pandora: "she who has [brings] all gifts." Though the text defines the woes she spreads as "banes" ($\lambda\upsilon\gamma\rho\dot{\alpha}$) and never as gifts, she provides men, just as her name suggests, with all sorts of inevitable, unwanted, and unnecessary "gift-banes" ($\delta\tilde{\omega}\rho\alpha$). She is both the carrier and the bestower of all the evils and remedies that represent the process of "culture." This divine gift, then, given by all the gods and all-giving to men, forms the receptacle which at once receives and returns everything ($\pi\acute{\alpha}\nu\delta o\kappa o\varsigma$ and $\pi\acute{\alpha}\nu\delta\omega\rho o\varsigma$). Some centuries later Plato will describe with an analogous set of *oxymora* the third $\epsilon\tilde{\iota}\delta o\varsigma$, which consists of neither the eternal ideas nor that which is imitated and is always moving.[39] This reference does not imply any relationship between Pandora and Plato's cryptical *chora* but simply shows how Pandora presents in her name itself the qualifications that place her on no one side. Thus, her name predicates a special position which makes her origin and non-origin, nurse and nurtured, life giving and life-taking.

On this last point—that Pandora is the carrier of death—we have already dwelt. Yet we should explore the possibility that the text may be alluding to her funereal function when Hermes (who, by naming her, takes on the function of a father) leads her to Epimetheus. Here Hermes acts under the suggestion of Zeus (see $\pi\acute{\epsilon}\mu\pi\epsilon$ [84]); he is especially suited to this task, for he is the messenger of the gods. But more precisely, as the ancients already felt, he can act as the leader of souls to Hades. In fact, the epithet used here for Hermes, διάκτορος (paraphrased in *Od.* 24. 100 by ψυχὰς κατάγων, "leading down the souls") suggested to Nessos Hermes' fatal role (Pertusi *Scholia Vetera* 77c =Diels Kranz, *Die Vors.* 69 B 2);

> Νέσσος ὁ Χίων ⟨διάκτορον λέγει⟩ ἀπὸ τοῦ διάγειν
> τὰς τῶν τελευτώντων ψυχάς.
> Nessos from Chios says that *diaktoros* comes from
> leading the souls of the dead.

If this sense was felt by the poet and the ancient audience, Pandora might have been represented in a fatal journey, accompanied by the god who also plays the role of her social father.[40]

The "symbolic" representation of Pandora receives a definite reinforcement from Aphrodite's helpers and from Hermes. Let us consider her other attributes. Hephaistos "*shapes* her from earth" and makes her "similar to a modest virgin following the will of Zeus" (70-71). Unlike the phrasing of Zeus's command ("*mix* earth with water"), our text stresses form rather than matter. But the most striking novelty is the lack of any reference to the goddesses whom Pandora should resemble. She emerges as a standardized virgin, a copy of a copy. She is removed from the awesome proximity of the goddesses,[41] from the position of the first copy. Pandora is no longer recognizable as an imitation of the goddesses unless we give a precise and strong sense to the phrase "following the will of Zeus" (Κρονίδεω διὰ βουλάς).[42] In addition, Athena does not carry out her father's orders exactly. Instead of teaching Pandora a new craft, she simply dresses Pandora.[43] While the shift from teaching to dressing is perhaps not as inexplicable as it first appears,[44] the verb ʒῶσε used in the text evokes Pandora's virginity (ʒώνη) instead of recalling the craft of weaving.

Finally, Hermes, who gives Pandora a symbolic name, bestows on her "lies and crafty talk" (ψεύδεά θ' αἱμυλίους τε λόγους), which explicitly designate *language*. Zeus, however, had conceived "a bitch's mind." The shift should be clear: Hermes confers upon Pandora the "signs" or "tokens" or "expression" of the "bitch's mind." But, again, something tamer and gentler is attributed to Pandora. One has only to look at the kinds of actions described as "bitchy" or "shameless" in the epos (Agamemnon dishonoring Achilles in *Il.* 9. 373; Helen betraying Menelaos in *Il.* 3. 180; Clytemnestra's murder of Agamemnon in *Od.* 11. 424 ff.) to appreciate Hermes' gentler touch.

Our analysis has shown a coherent new feature in the gods' manufacture of Pandora: the attributes that Zeus conceived for Pandora are in part translated and materialized in tokens, signs, and symbols of those attributes. Pandora emerges deprived of the violent, bewildering power and presence of the gods and appears as a copy of a copy, an "image" of a figure.

The symbolic quality of Pandora is in keeping with the emergence of time and change. Spring flowers adorn Pandora's wreath: in the abstract atemporality in which the drama has been acted out, we suddenly perceive a change of season. And human beauty from now on is to be more and more identified with age and represented as the only divine season of man, his spring.

Pandora's spring flowers may symbolize the blossoming (the beginning) of the human race. Spring is typically the season of bloom both in Hesiod and Homer (see *Il.* 6. 148). Spring flowers, similarly, might imply that Pandora is, like spring, "blossoming" and "bounteous"; and, in this case, the symbolism would contradict Hesiod's interpretation of Pandora's name.[45]

As the gods manufacture Pandora, she emerges as an imitation of something, as a token and a sign-carrier of something, but she is deprived of the awesome, godlike imprint that might have made her the close copy and apprentice of the gods that Zeus had conceived of. Even then she would have been a sign, but a sign closer to its referent, more marked by the presence of its "signified." Now the distance between Pandora and her model has been increased: her relation to the original has grown faded, both because it is almost effaced in the text and because it is represented by symbolic elements such as her ornaments or her name. The symbolic "representation" of Pandora teaches us that the process of mimesis, of copying, produces an uncontrollable extension, diffusion, and proliferation of signifiers, of meanings, and of signs. Even the gods, facing the "copy" that Zeus ordered them to manufacture, "interpreted"; and their interpretation—Pandora—is both the result of their "reading" of Zeus's copy and the embodiment of new signs and signifiers. In her final version, Pandora becomes the reproduction of a "figura," an expansion, multiplication, and dissemination of figurative elements, while the "original" grows less and less distinct. But we know that the "original" has, in fact, no origin; it has always assumed the posture of a replacement and has been evoked only by a copy, a sign, by language.

A second point should be made. The elaborate symbolism of the text, and especially the etymological explanation of Pandora's name, implies a "rhetorical" creation of Pandora by Hesiod. Pandora emerges as the first human being and as the first rhetorical "figure" as well. Because of her symbolic function and, literally, because of her ornaments and flowers, her glamor and her scheming mind, Pandora emblematizes the beginning of rhetoric; but at the same time she also stands for the rhetoric of the beginning. For she is both the "figure" of the origin and the origin of the "figure"—the first being invested with symbolic, referential, rhetorical elements. The text implies both the human dawn unmarked by imitation and rhetoric and a turning point that initiates the beautifying, imi-

tative, rhetorical process. In this way, the text reproduces the split between
a language identical to reality and a language imitative of reality.

The evocation of an origin accommodates various intentions of Hesiod's
text. At the level that concerns us here, the myth of the origin of rhetoric implies a precedent moment in which language was straight and true. And since
the discovery of the origin as a turning point admits hope, and the possibility
of a reversal, the text intimates the possibilities of truthfulness in language
and of identity with the word of the gods. However, since demonstration of
the origin necessarily coincides with a rhetoric of the origin, Hesiod's language
has no chance of transcending rhetoric.

At the social and anthropological level as well, the myth of an origin as the
turning point that initiates history implies the possibility of a reversal. As we
shall see, this possibility is concretized in the golden age that blesses the City
of Justice (*Erga* 227 ff.).

We have seen that Pandora constitutes the transition from the golden age to
our own corrupt time; thus, it is understandable that the text should heighten
her total negativity. Like the crooked, deflecting, false, imitative *logos*, she
stands at the opposite pole of what is straight, identical, and good. But here
again, this separation and opposition suits only the edifying force and meaning
of the text. As we have seen, Pandora functions as a "figure" and an impersonation of that imitative process which leads to sameness through differing, pro-
tracting, and deferring movement. She is, therefore, that which allows the establishment of oppositions, and in fact, she appears to us as both origin and the
non-origin, as a gift given by all and as she who gives all; she carries death that
replaces natural sleep, beauty that looks like that of the goddesses, and so on.
In this way, she personifies the structure of replacement that, by replacing, representing, etc., constitutes the non-original "matrix" of oppositions.

ZEUS AND PANDORA

As we approach the third act of the myth, we shall test the consistency of
our interpretation. For whether Zeus is really absent from the scene—as many
interpreters maintain—or whether Pandora acts only as a weapon of Zeus's
arsenal, the text emphasizes the activity of one agent over the other. Given
our interpretation, however, how could the moment of identity or that of
the copy be preeminent? Is not identity comprehensible only in terms of the
movement of difference and deferment? In other words, if Pandora is a mere
token of Zeus, and if Zeus is present and active at the fatal moment, then Pandora plays only a secondary role, as a fabulous element introduced to enliven
the narrative. In this case, Zeus controls everything, and the introduction of
death and other toils for men is not left to Pandora's whim, or to chance,

but may be traced back to Zeus's decision to punish Prometheus's disloyalty.

On the other hand, it may be argued that if Pandora has been created as
an independent person, fully aware of her actions, Zeus himself is left in
the background. Pandora then is acting as a "typically" mythical character:
her gesture, unmotivated as it seems, explains, through the "logic" of myth,
that which is unexplainable. The reader will here recognize the two main critical interpretations of the story of Pandora. Each singles out one of the two
principal roles and eliminates the responsibility of one of the protagonists.
In my opinion, it is only in recognizing the complementarity of the two
characters and the simultaneity of their action that we can reach a consistent
interpretation that respects the text.

We shall now explore Zeus's and Pandora's responsibility at the crucial
moment of the lifting of the lid from the vase. Pandora is described as acting
of her own will (ἐμήσατο κήδεα λυγρά 95); she lifts the big lid (μέγα πῶμ')
with her own hands (94), far away from Zeus (especially if line 99 is to be
bracketed) since the jar is presumably stored in Epimetheus's house.

Tracing the signs of Zeus's presence around the fatal vase, we first recall
that Pandora is, in a peculiar way, the daughter of Zeus, and that the text
of the *Theogony*, if it is sound, refers to woman in exactly that way (Διὸς . . .
ὑπέδεκτο . . . παρθένον [*Th*. 514 ff.]).[46] Moreover, we recall that Pandora
is created as a new weapon of Zeus's strategy against Prometheus.[47] In fact,
line 95, which describes Pandora's independent and nasty decision, merely
repeats line 49, where Zeus prepares blows against mortals. What is more,
Zeus is mentioned twice as being present, once at the opening of the vase (99)
and once in an unspecified occasion immediately after the opening of the vase
(104). Let us begin with line 104, which has never raised any suspicions, either
because of its cryptic nature or the supposed innocence of its meaning. Here
Zeus, present and active, takes language away from the diseases that Pandora
has spread all around; he acts brutally, for he perfects the destructiveness of
Pandora's gesture. By depriving the diseases of language Zeus makes them
"*automatoi*" (103) and therefore untouchable by human *logos*, persuasion,
control, and deferment. This point becomes clear when we recall the plague
that befalls the Greeks in the first book of the *Iliad*: the disease has a namable
cause, Agamemnon's insolence against Chryses, as well as a namable divine
agent, Apollo. By placating the priest and his god with due prayers and sacri-
fices, the disease is removed. This plague is neither "automatos" (coming of
its own will) not speechless, for Apollo is invited, even begged, by his own
priest to intervene, and the arrows themselves emit a sound as they fall. Now,
however, Zeus withdraws the diseases from the control and the deferment of
logos; he makes them "automatoi," thereby creating the ultimate bane for

men, for Zeus's intervention causes the situation to become irreparable. Consequently, he perfects the destructiveness of Pandora's act.

In line 99 Zeus bids Pandora to put the lid on the jar before Elpis (Hope/Fear) can get out (98–99). Without line 99, one would assume that Pandora replaces the lid of her own accord, leaving it to the imagination of the reader to provide a motivation for such a gesture. Wilamowitz, for instance, has suggested that the girl becomes frightened and closes the vase. But why must we look for hypothetical motivations when the text states one: Zeus's will? Many interpreters choose to preserve the "authenticity" of the fable by athetizing the inconvenient line, since it introduces the heavy shadow of theology. It appears that interpreters may wish at this point to dissociate the majesty of Zeus from the silly gestures of his undignified creature: this might well be why the indirect tradition of the Hellenistic period does not transmit line 99, whereas all the manuscripts contain it. In my opinion, the text is sound; but it is, after all, possible to understand the neglect of such a line by people like Plutarch.[48] We read Zeus's desire for Elpis to remain in the jar as an act that enables man to endure a situation otherwise insufferable: for as death and disease become *automatoi*, only Elpis can help man endure life.

In opposition to the tendency of the critics to reduce the complicity of Zeus and Pandora to one unique role by suppressing the presence and the responsibility of the other partner, I believe that the text itself intimates the complementarity and complicity of the two characters. Indeed, the above-mentioned critical tendencies conspire with the obvious duplicity of the text; they are not "invented" by the critics. In suppressing one of the characters of this fatal action, we are saving a metaphysical principle. Thus, for instance, by assuming that Zeus controls everything,[49] we may preserve the theological principle that the world is controlled by the rationality—however difficult to understand—of Zeus; on the other hand, by suppressing the presence and responsibility of Zeus, the text would suggest a fabulous explanation of that which cannot be rationally explained (see Wilamowitz, note 48). Zeus's reputation and majesty would be saved.

Zeus and Pandora, however, act together, simultaneously and complementarily: the "original" and the "copy" collaborate in one action, creating a new figure of difference. Pandora, as token of Zeus, and Zeus, as the original maker of Pandora, each takes on a unique role and task: the imitation embraces the original so that lie and truth, death and immortality are not strangers, separate and distinct, but accomplices, moving together in a vortex that at once distinguishes and blurs them.

Even from a strictly literary point of view, the force and the impact of this text derive from an irresolvable tension and vibration between the two characters—so opposite yet so alike—and from the unity and complicity of polarized oppositions: Pandora's levity and Zeus's divine consciousness, the total arbitrariness of their gesture and the tremendous necessity that commands it. Thus, Pandora takes on some of Zeus's power, and Zeus is marked by some of Pandora's levity: the movement of the action combines them in a vortex which is at once a playful game and the ultimate evil.

ELPIS

In comparison with the *Theogony*, where the coming of death is balanced by the remedy of the immortality of the family (*Th.* 602-10), the coming of death in the *Erga* elicits a more theological, cosmic, and bitter view of man's destiny. Pandora's jar emits all its demoniacal evils and diseases,[50] while Zeus detains Elpis inside the jar and mercilessly condemns man's life by depriving diseases of their language:

> Only Elpis remained there, inside the unbreakable
> room under the lips of the jar and did not flee
> forth . . . But other ten thousand evils wander
> among men. For the earth is full of evils and the
> sea as well is full of evils. And by day and by
> night diseases visit men, moving by their own will
> (αὐτόματοι) bringing evils to the mortals,
> silently, since Zeus the wise has taken away their
> voice.
>
> (*Erga* 96-104)

The ἄλλα of ἄλλα . . . μυρία λυγρά (100) proves that Elpis (Hope and Fear at once[51]) is itself considered a bane; this should not surprise us. For Elpis, as the wishful or fearful anticipation of the future, marks the fall of man, appearing on the human scene of identity and happiness along with the various other forms of disease—work, toil, etc.

The questions raised by Elpis—why she remains inside, to what purpose, and so on—have always fascinated critics. I would, in turn, propose an interpretation that , while not fully resolving the problem, might help to elucidate some aspects of it. Inasmuch as she is a "daimon" in the jar, consorting with other evil "daimons" and ready to follow them out, Elpis is a potentially disastrous evil. If, as happens to the diseases, Elpis were deprived of the *logos*, man might be pushed to total insanity, for an "automatos" Elpis would create sheer havoc. By remaining inside the jar, therefore, Elpis does not run this risk, and she preserves her language.

Consequently, since Elpis is essentially a speaking being, a goddess of some sort, she can also listen to men's words. Thus, for instance, in *Erga* 498, Hesiod discourages Perses from trusting Elpis, for "an idle man who rests in view of

vain Elpis [or "who remains near a vain Elpis"[52]] addresses many bad words
to himself in his heart[53] when he needs food. And Elpis is a bad companion
for the man in need who sits in an idle place, when he has no sufficient livelihood." Given Hesiod's view of language, we expect, of course, that the language of Elpis must be vain (κενεήν . . . ἐλπίδα [498]) and the companionship
of such a *logos* negative (οὐκ ἀγαθή [500]), for Elpis speaks of the future
and of distant things, and her *logos* therefore cannot be similar or equal to
these things, or go straight to them. The difference between the *logos* of Elpis
and truth is obvious and demonstrable. For this reason, the man whom Elpis
accompanies sits ἐν λέσχῃ, in a "lounging place," the place for idle chatter.[54]
A few lines earlier (493) this place is described as warm and sunny[55] in winter-
time (ἐπαλέα λέσχην [493]); it is therefore a delusive place that softens
reality, offering warmth "when cold prevents man from work." This voice of
Elpis is indeed an accomplice of man's poverty, need, and hunger.

But Elpis can also have a good voice and propose positive discourse. This
presumably happens at line 273, where Hesiod ceases to despair of Zeus's
absence and states his hope: ἀλλὰ τά γ'οὔ πω ἔολπα τελεῖν Δία μητιόεντα.
As we have seen, a moment of despair at the poor administration of justice
follows the installation of Dikê by the throne of Zeus. Unexpectedly, the
voice of Hope intervenes; the voice is presumably good because it arises when
true and straight discourse absents itself, replacing that discourse and, in a way,
becoming its ally. Analogously, in *Erga* 475 Hesiod hopes that his brother may
have the joy of having enough stored food within his house. This hope continues, and it anticipates the result toward which the whole discourse of the *Erga*
aims.

The *logos* of Elpis, therefore, is an additional *logos*, as the metaphor of the
"companion" suggests; and it becomes alternately an accomplice of the crooked
logos or an ally of the straight one. By itself, the discourse of Elpis is without
grounds and far from truth, tending toward emptiness and vanity. Rising beside
the true and straight *logos*, supporting it, replacing it when this *logos* absents
itself, it becomes good discourse. When, however, the *logos* of Elpis allies itself
to the chatter in the lounging place, and rises to sustain it, then Elpis's words
form a bad *logos*.[56]

The suggestion that a remedy might possibly exist does not alter the fact
that the ultimate disaster falls silently on the human scene. Death descends
over men day and night, carried by silent demons in their inevitable visitation.

PANDORA OUTSIDE AND INSIDE THE HOUSE

As the myth of Pandora ends, the fatal bane has descended on man. A happy
world is lost and in its place a fully reversed state emerges. Here we may sum-
marize briefly all the opposite, polar terms that have been implied in the long story:

Godlike man	Woman resembling the goddesses
Identity	Imitation, copy
Symmetry	Addition, excess, loss
Natural birth from earth	Manufacture with earth and water
No reproduction, unicity	Sexuality, reproduction
Spontaneity	Artifice, art, toil
Truth	Falsity
Natural sleep	Diseases, death

Some of these oppositions may appear too sketchy when reduced to labels intended for convenient presentation, but they must all be understood in their more profound context. Thus, for instance, the first opposition—Godlike man : Woman resembling the goddesses—implies, as we have seen, man close to the gods versus a humanity forever separated from the gods, with all the ensuing contrasts (banquet with the gods versus sacrifice, etc.). Analogously, the male born from the earth constitutes a completely different specimen of man from that born of woman. The introduction of the female implies sex and family—both previously unknown to man.

The set of oppositions we have uncovered indicates what we have called the *edifying* intentions of the text, which we shall now examine more closely. The terms of the two columns represent, in general, ideal values as opposed to facts of real human life. The ideal values of the left column suggest an agrarian utopia, as is evident in the passage in which Hesiod describes the assets of the city that honors Justice (Dikè [225 ff.]). Since the straight Dikè comes from Zeus, the relationship with the gods is a close one: Zeus bestows peace, and feasting returns. (θαλίης [231]). Earth produces an abundant livelihood, and aspects of the golden age reappear, both in the generosity of earth (232-34) and in the self-sufficiency that divine earth grants to man (236-37).

The spontaneous production of the earth in the City of Justice is represented in expressions that recall the golden age; in both cases, it is not easy to understand exactly what "work" implies (119 and 231), since fruits are prodigiously abundant. At any rate, the similarity of the expressions does suggest an almost complete return to the blessings of the golden age.

Furthermore, a sort of identity is reinstated in the City of Justice, for women bear children truly similar to their fathers (ἐοικότα τέκνα γονεῦσιν [235]). Women no longer introduce a difference in the male lineage of the family. Though they obviously come to males from other families, their reproductive function does not alter the resemblance of the children to the father.[57] This prodigious effect reestablishes identity: while in the golden age this identity was characteristic of each male, in the City of Justice it is attributed to the descendants, who endlessly repeat the father.

Finally, temporal change ceases. Here again, as in the golden age, a kind of immutability prevails, and men enjoy their good fortune continuously, eternally (διαμπερές [236]).

The song that the Muses sing, which is true, i.e., identical to things as they are, envisages the return of a certain identity and posits a real possibility of suppressing the difference, just as the Muses actually have suppressed the difference in their song for the poet.

If we interpret the text in this way, the coherence of its construction becomes apparent: the metaphysical motions of repetition without difference, of spontaneous gifts, of flowing presence of Earth and Gods mark Hesiod's utopian world and create a transparent unity that encompasses various aspects of this world: poetry and justice, agriculture and social life. Transgressing all the limits of and differences between these various aspects, Hesiod recovers their underlying unity in those qualities that characterize his own language; namely, its identity with the things as they are, its ability to repeat things without any difference, its divine origin and ascendancy.

The difference, however, exists: the Muses may recount things and events with distortions that cannot be proved, and Pandora has introduced deceitful imitation among men. Though Hesiod is aware of this, his myth assumes that a split or a fence exists between a mode of repetition without difference (identity) and a mode of repetition with difference (simulation of identity, corrupted imitation). Both modes of repetition are contiguous, since they are comprehended by the same notion of imitation (ὁμοῖα), but the myth introduces a reassuring distance in order to separate them.

The "mythical" narrative, in contrast with the "logos," guarantees this distance, this chasm: when dikê becomes Dikê she can sing her protest in a reassuring setting, by the throne of her father Zeus, no longer pierced by the claws of the hawk. Analogously, though inversely, Pandora's imitation removes the gods from the human scene and opens a chasm between identity and difference.

Yet our analysis has described Pandora as an *oxymoron* and has elucidated the precariousness of the univocal role, that of evil, she plays in the narrative. Pandora as a "figure" of difference should be thought of as the "matrix" of the opposition, not as its negative pole.

We now can analyze what happens to Pandora when she is removed from the mythical realm and is introduced into everyday life as a normal woman and wife. Hesiod discusses the nature and the value of woman in several passages of his texts, either in picturesque similes and metaphors or in straight precepts. We will see, first of all, that Pandora concretely realizes the function we have attributed to her in the myth; namely, that of replacing the previous conditions of life by merely imitating them. In fact, she brings back these conditions, but they are faded and incomplete, and she does so only through a painful and endless movement of detour.

Furthermore, Hesiod can no longer classify the woman as an evil: he is forced also to accept her as a good of some sort. The oxymoronic nature of the mythical Pandora is here unraveled in a contradictory statement: we will see how Hesiod resolves it.

In the *Theogony*, the creation of the woman is followed by the observation that she represents ruin for the poor household. Yet men are almost forced to marry, for Zeus

> bestowed a second evil instead of a blessing. He
> who escapes marriage and the awful works of women
> and does not want to get married comes to old age
> without anyone to tend his old age. He has no
> lack of livelihood while he lives, but as he dies,
> relatives divide his possessions.
>
> (*Th*. 602-7)

In a short and extremely cryptic statement ("Zeus bestowed a second evil"), the text provides a glimpse into the extent of the disaster introduced by woman. Before she appeared, men evidently did not grow old, did not need to accumulate possessions, and were presumably overcome by death as if by sleep. But woman carries within herself all diseases and death, the troubles and toils of social life, and the necessity for prudent saving. As a result, when the unmarried man dies, no son will be there to tend him and all his savings, and his possessions will be divided up among relatives (χηρωσταί).[58] In this precise connection, the woman plays a paradoxical role: on the one hand, she is the bearer of death, on the other, she insures the continuity of a father's house. She is at once the ruin of the household and the guarantee of its preservation beyond the short season of a man's vigor.

In an extended simile (*Th*. 594 ff.), Hesiod maintains that women are bad for men, that they are no help in poverty, but only in abundance. The simile equates women with drones and men with bees:

> In the roofed hives bees feed the drones, who
> are conspirators in evil works; and while bees
> work zealously all day, the drones, remaining
> (ἔντοσθε μένοντες) within the roofed hives,
> reap the toil of others (ἀλλότριον κάματον) in
> their bellies. Just so, high thundering Zeus
> made women, conspirators in evil works, to be a
> bane to men.

The woman is the natural companion (σύμφοροι[592]), ally, and lover of Abundance.[59] The alliance and love, here and in other places, is seen disapprovingly as motivated by woman's rapaciousness (she is "like a thief" [*Erga* 375]) or by her gluttony (*Erga* 704).

Women, sitting where they do not belong, inside the houses of men, appropriate and waste the property of others, the fruit of others' labor. They contradict, therefore, the principle of gathering wealth, which depends on the patient accumulation of things inside the house, brought in little by little from outside (*Erga* 361).

Consistent with the whole Pandora story, the woman, like a drone, enters from the outside as a different being, as a gratuitous, superfluous addition to the male's house, as a perverse gift sent by Zeus and accepted by the foolish Epimetheus. The woman moves in a space still unmarked by any limits and marks it with an inside and an outside. Though space cannot be imagined without some delimitation, before Pandora's appearance men lived "far from evils" (*Erga* 91, 113). This unique spatial determination in the description of the golden race evokes no spatial tension in terms of inside : outside; however, when woman appears, space is marked. Men, too, occasionally turn to the wealth of others (*Erga* 33–34) or are compared to drones when they live in idleness (*Erga* 303 ff.): in that case they are unjust and violent, destroying the principle of dikè. But these villains are only a degenerate specimen of the whole race which, before Pandora, was wholly just and blessed; while women, because of their origin, are by nature and constitution unjust, foreign, thieving (*Erga* 375), and capable of tricking men with lies and deception:

> Let not the flaunting woman deceive your mind
> with flattering and scheming words: she aims at your
> barn. Who trusts a woman trusts a thief.
>
> (*Erga* 373–75)

Whatever πυγοστόλος means[60] (we translate it by "flaunting," with Evelyn-White) it directly evokes the force of sex: the "charis" of Aphrodite and the more urbane and polite expressions of *Erga* 73 ff. are left behind.

All these attributes of woman make her an enemy of Dikè, of agriculture, of the true song. In fact, not only does woman come "flaunting," she also comes armed with the tricks and the lies of Hermes (compare αἱμύλα κωτίλλουσα [374] with *Erga* 78: ψεύδεά θ' αἱμυλίους λόγους). We have already touched upon the relationship between the work of Dikè and agricultural activity. M. Detienne, in *Crise agraire*, has convincingly shown the correspondence between the two realms. I should like to add a point regarding the identification of the voice of Dikè as a projection of the voice of the poet. Let us see how Hesiod describes the process of accumulation of wealth in the house of the farmer:

For even if you should add little to little and do
it often, soon even that would be great. He who
adds to what is there shall escape fiery hunger.
What a man has stored at home does not trouble him:
it is better to have the substance at home, since what is
outside is ruinous. And it is good to take from
what is there; on the contrary, it is a bane to
desire in one's heart what is absent. I bid you
to think about these points.

                                                    (*Erga* 361–67)

This passage occurs toward the end of the section devoted to the moral be-
havior of a just and fair farmer: in a few lines the poet advises Perses to beget one child and to work hard in order to achieve wealth. This passage is
remarkable for its style. The hoarding, the goods, the food, and their op-
posites are described six times by the most abstract and general kind of
expressions (substantivate participles: ἐπ᾿ ἐόντι [363], τὸ κατακείμενον [364],
παρεόντος [366], ἀπεόντος [367] and substantivate adjectives or adverbs:
ὀμικρόν [361], τὸ θύρηφιν [365]). The hoarding of the food is defined as
"what is there, present, stored inside" and pitted against what is outside,
absent, hidden under the earth (42). The process of the production of wealth
amounts to restoring what has been lost through a toiling process, and to
bringing inside and piling up what has been so restored. The door of the house
is the *limen* that separates presence, goodness, and abundance, from absence,
evil, and hunger.

   Analogously, Perses should lay up in his heart, store in his mind, and keep
present in his memory the voice of his brother Hesiod singing about Dikè and
the true things told to him by the Muses. Here, at line 367, Hesiod commands
his brother (ἅ σε φράσεσθαι ἄνωγα) with an Odyssean formula (φράσεσθαι
ἄνωγα [*Od.* 1. 269]); at other times, Hesiod bids his brother to remember, to
"put in his memory" (298, 616 etc.) or to store in his mind (σὺ δὲ ταῦτα
τεῷ ἐνικάτθεο θυμῷ [27]; see also 107, 274, etc.). If we recall our analysis
of Hesiod's poetry as a gift, we realize here how the same metaphysical concept lies behind the analogy between poetry and property. The truth of
Hesiod's poem is offered as a gift to Perses, to be stored inside along with
the other plentiful goods of life. Similarly, the presence of truth and the
presence of property—of what is "own"—are acquired in like ways; the presence of truth implies the repression of the difference as otherness (the achievement of an identity with things); the presence of property is likewise obtained
by repressing the exteriority (or "outsidedness") of things.

The exteriority, the deviousness, of woman are therefore in opposition to the series of terms that evoke the presence of wealth, of dikè, and of truth. The woman moves inside the house, with a wreath of flowers on her head, squandering the accumulated wealth and taking on the posture of otherness. The wreath of flowers, the rhetoric of her deviousness, the "glamor" of her beauty, the colors of her dress—all these attributes of Pandora constitute manipulations of truth and of presence, signs which evoke that which is not there: forms of waste and dissipation, assaults on the self and its autonomy. Therefore, the coherence of the straight and true *logos* commands the condemnation of Pandora and her exclusion from the center of the house, from the center of the accumulation of wealth, and from the center of the self and the mind.

What escapes this *logos*, however, is the process of difference. As the abundance of the golden age can only be achieved through the painful process of work and through patient accumulation, rigorous economic control, restraint in enjoyment, and moderation in festivals, difference and deferral are again at play. The plentitude of food *cannot* be obtained by a divine fiat as Hesiod obtains divine truth from the Muses. Indeed, creation of abundance is rather to be compared with the slow process of the composition of Hesiod's text.

Yet if the plenty of the golden age begins with the accumulation of wealth inside the house, the woman must be at once a threat and a resource. For reasons good or bad, woman is installed inside the house, and without her protection and her childbearing to insure the permanence of the house, the whole project amounts to naught.[61] Thus, however contradictorily, the text must make room for woman on the grounds that she is the childbearer and can be assimilated to man's project: she can be appropriated as a possession and she can learn man's ways and become like him. Thus her outsideness and otherness can be mastered.

As Hesiod concludes the section of his poem devoted to the moral attributes of the good farmer, he advises Perses to beget only one child. Although woman has not yet been mentioned, the need for her is here implied:

> May there be an only born son to feed his father's
> house, for in this way wealth will increase in the
> halls. May death take you late while you leave
> another son.[62]
>
> (*Erga* 376–78)

The entire house must feed only one child, and he in turn must feed the ancestral house.[63] The father figure looms like that of a god: a god of the ancestral lineage and of the continuation of the house in which all sons are only instruments.[64]

And, finally, woman herself appears:

> In the flower of your age lead home your bride. . . .
> Marry a virgin so that you may teach her good ways.
> Marry a neighbor best of all,
> looking carefully around you [read with the manuscript's
> ἀμφὶς ἰδών—see also Wilamowitz, p. 120], lest your
> marriage become a joke to your neighbors.
> For no better prey does a man win than a good wife. . . .
>
> (*Erga* 695 ff.)

The woman is taken *inside* a man's house (τεὸν ποτὶ οἶκον ἄγεσθαι) to be
changed from an "other" into something like man himself. For teaching her
good ways means making her like man, that is, without any difference.65
The man must be about thirty years old and the woman much younger (four
years after puberty, 696-97), and she must be a virgin to insure her receptivity
to the teaching of good ways. Her physical virginity parallels her spiritual receptivity to the imprint of the master. She has to live in the *neighborhood* in order
to be familiar to her prospective husband. And finally, if she is good, she is the
best booty (ληΐζετ') for man. The woman is no longer a ruinous addition, a
kakon to be embraced, an unsolicited gift accepted by foolish Epimetheus;
appropriated like booty, she loses the dangerous quality of outsideness equated
with the threatening posture of the uninvited drone. The ring-composition built
up through the opposition of man's and woman's attributes is undone. The il-
legitimacy of woman's position inside the house ends when she is assimilated by
man as his property, imitating his ways.

With the advent of Pandora, the world of identity and plenitude has dis-
appeared, and in its place a series of detours, differences, and deferrals moves
in. Since Pandora, embodying this process, continues to threaten all attempts
at restoring identity and plenitude, the movement of difference must be mastered by repressing the difference in Pandora herself. Only in this way can the
inside of the house become that space in which the accumulation of wealth,
dikè, and truth may point to a reinstatement of the golden age; that is, the
City of Justice. Consequently, woman is accepted inside the house, but accepted only as man's property and as his pupil, in order to efface her inherent difference, her otherness, and her outsideness.

We recognize the pattern: the difference lies behind the oppositional terms
"outside : inside," "other : self," and so on; Pandora is coherently shown to
be both the dangerous "outsideness" and the protective "insideness," the ruin
and the permanence of the home. But the text aims at controlling the contiguity
of these terms and at mastering their baffling tension. To this end, Hesiod tries
to master the difference by a double movement, through which Pandora, as difference, is rejected as evil but is simultaneously accepted as the property and

imitation of man. The movement parallels that of the *imitation* which opens
false and crooked discourse, but which, when perfect (i.e., without difference)
can also open the discourse of truth.

It is also instructive to analyze the economy of this double movement. In
the *mythical* narration of Pandora's creation, the text in its explicit intention
masters the difference, embodied by Pandora, by placing her full negativity
within a structure of contrasts that opens a chasm, a split, a distance, between
identity and difference. This chasm is both temporal and local: Pandora displaces what existed *before*—which may also return in the future, in the City
of Justice—and removes the gods from humanity and humanity from godlike
life. In the description of everyday life, on the contrary, only the *limen* of
the house separates the negativity of Pandora from the goods inside the house:
in this case the difference embodied by Pandora cannot simply be bracketed and
pitted against the property and the presence of the goods; for the *limen* has already been transgressed by the woman. As a consequence, the myth elicits the
direct vision of a lost yet recoverable presence, identity, and fullness by introducing the possibility of keeping the difference away, by presenting as ideal
not the mastering of difference but the disappearance of difference. That is
why the mythical master of truth—with the exception of the Muses themselves—cannot claim to be a master of lies as well. Indeed, we have seen that
Pandora in the myth itself is the "matrix" of the opposition, rather than a
term of the opposition, but our uncovering of this role does not affect the
explicit intention of the myth.[66]

On the contrary, in the description of everyday life Pandora is *explicitly*
shown to function in an ambivalent way. The *limen* itself is the boundary
that the woman as a drone has transgressed and that the woman as a prey
carried inside the house by her conqueror has legitimately crossed. In this
case, when the space between good and evil does not guarantee any exclusion
of evil, the woman, the *kakon*, the difference, must be mastered: and it can
be mastered, in the intention of the text, by appropriating it. Man seizes her
as a booty, teaches her his ways, and forces upon her his control, his imprint,
and his signature.

We can now apply these conclusions to both the mythical and conceptual-
ized representations of poetry that we have discussed in the first chapter. We
have seen that the mythical representation of poetry as a divine gift from the
Muses allows Hesiod to recover the intact word of truth. The myth of Pandora,
by opening a chasm, a split, and a distance between the world of identity and
that of corrupted imitation, sustains that claim, for it separates what appeared
so dangerously contiguous in *Theogony* 27–28. Furthermore, the myth of the
divine gift of poetry represents the singer in direct contact with the breath of
the Muses: the myth, therefore, seems to discount the existence of a poetic

tradition and the "outsideness" of language. Not unlike what happens in the myth of Pandora, the myth of poetry brackets the difference, the false imitation, by placing it outside and removing it from the realm of identity. Indeed, we have seen that this project is contradicted, but the intentional aim of the myth is not affected by this contradiction.

On the contrary, as Hesiod prescribes the capture of a wife and the necessity of appropriating her, he sees that the difference cannot simply be bracketed, but must be bent and mastered. The analogy is again clear: the poet, too, must appropriate the poetic language, i.e., the language of other poets—which exists outside him, and which claims to be truthful although it is only simulation of truth—and he must force his own imprint and signature on this language as he does when he competes with other poets or assumes the protest of the victims of violence as his own song.

Accordingly, myth does not need to teach difference, to school and to appropriate it. When the Muses shock us with the tremendous ambiguity of their acknowledgment of the two discourses, they do not tell us how to distinguish between them or why they, who are present where all events occur, should simulate the truth. Presumably they are the masters of the difference and use it with deceptive intent, just as Zeus does when he invents Pandora and uses her deceptive imitation as a weapon against man's happiness. The gods, as masters of difference, can dispose of it in the mode of absence. This is the reassuring gesture of myth. Yet the text of the myth shows that not even the gods can master difference: the sweetly speaking Muses turn their words into poisonous insults and Zeus assumes a debasing role as accomplice to Pandora.

That the myth disposes of the difference and, accordingly, does not use a *techne* in trying to appropriate and control it constitutes both its force and its weakness in relation to the *logos*. These remarks receive support by Jurij Lotman's and Boris A. Uspenskij's view that myth speaks essentially through names—in contrast to nouns—and is, therefore, denominational: by indicating things with their *nom propre*, myth in principle denies the sign-quality of language and aims at an identity or consistency of words with their referent. (Mif-Imja-Kul'tura, translated into Italian by D. Ferrari Bravo, in *Semeiotica e Cultura*, Milano Napoli 1975, pp. 99 ff). In this way, myth aims at disposing of the difference of language, as if this difference were simply non-existent in the myth's own language.

The myth of Pandora and the precepts that Hesiod gives about marriage aim at the same result, the control of the difference, though each proceeds through a different economy and strategy. This difference creates an additional tension in the text of the *Erga*. Since Pandora has a scheming mind and is herself defined as a trick (δόλος), the appropriation of the woman as a booty and her schooling are never definitive and radical enough. Especially when the period introduced by her is compared to the ideal golden age, Pandora always appears as a loss rather than a gain, notwithstanding the effacement of her otherness and outsideness. In fact, even in the luckiest and best marriages the woman symbolizes the fall, so that even for the man "who gets a good wife, provided with good sense . . . evil constantly contends with good." (*Th.* 607-10). Here the text repeats a situation characteristic of the iron age (*Erga* 179; see also p. 63). For the woman remains token and quintessence of the iron race, while man, in his common origin and life with the gods, represents the golden race. If, then, the woman acts as a remedy in the new situation she has created, this happens in defiance of her "true" nature—in Hesiod's eyes—yet in accordance with her real role as difference and deferral.

The most important reference books and papers for this chapter are the following:

Detienne, M. *Crise agraire et attitude religieuse chez Hésiode.* Collection "Latomus," vol. 68. Brussels-Berchem, 1963. (Hereafter cited as *Crise agraire.*)

Fink, G. "Pandora und Epimetheus: Mythologische Studien." Ph.D. dissertation, Erlangen, 1958. (Hereafter cited as Fink.)

Heitsch, E. "Das Prometheus-Gedicht bei Hesiod." *Rheinisches Museum* 1963, pp. 1-15. (Hereafter cited as Heitsch.)

Krafft, F. *Vergleichende Untersuchungen zu Homer und Hesiod.* Göttingen, 1963. (Hereafter cited as Krafft.)

Lendle, O. *Die 'Pandorasage' bei Hesiod.* Würzburg, 1957. (Hereafter cited as Lendle.)

Robert, C. "Pandora." *Hermes* 49 (1914): 17-38 (Hereafter cited as Robert.)

NOTES

1.   I would like to say a few words on the stance I have taken concerning the authenticity of the passage (lines 69-82) in the *Erga*. I am of the same opinion as those who consider the passage to be, on the whole, sound: C. Robert ("Pandora," *Hermes* 49 [1914]: 17-38); A. Lesky (review of H. Türck's *Pandora und Eva, Gnomon* 9 [1933]: 174); W. A. Oldfather (*Pauly's Realencyclopädie der Classischen Altertüms-wissenschaft*, vol. 18, pt. 3 [1949], s.v. "Pandora"); Colonna (in his text he brackets only 93); H. Erbse (review of O. Lendle's *Die 'Pandorasage' bei Hesiod, Gymnasium* 66 [1959]: 561 ff.); G. Fink ("Pandora und Epimetheus," Ph.D. dissertation, Erlangen, 1958); J. H. Kühn (review of O. Lendle's *Die 'Pandorasage' bei Hesiod, Gnomon* 31

[1959] : 114-23); E. Heitsch ("Das Prometheus-Gedicht bei Hesiod,"
Rheinisches Museum 1963, pp. 1-15); and others.

My analysis will add, I hope, some evidence in favor of this position. It would
be interesting to enter into a discussion of the methodological problems that a
text like the *Erga* poses, but such a discussion cannot be undertaken here.

2.   See West, p. 307: "What we have in Hesiod, then, is a combination of three
myths, all probably traditional, which could have been told separately, though
we cannot prove that they ever were."

3.   The object of ἔκρυψε should be understood as βίον from line 42. The narrative is difficult and compressed because it traces, in a regressive motion, the
motivations for the creation of Pandora and consequently, the necessity of
toil. I understand the passage thus: "Now the gods keep man's livelihood hidden (42). [But it was not always so.] For Zeus once hid it (47) when he was
deceived by Prometheus (48) and had, as a consequence of that deceit, conceived baneful plans (49). [He was deceived by Prometheus when] Zeus had
hidden fire (50) and Prometheus had stolen it from men (50 ff.). At this point
Zeus had turned to Prometheus and said (53). . . . "

The aim of Zeus is the same—only the means are different: first the deprivation of fire, then the sending of Pandora, and with her, the concealing of man's
livelihood and the necessity of toil (*Erga* 63 and 100).

4.   Νόσφιν ἄτερ is an un-Homeric formula. The repetition of this formula in
Hesiod's text suggests that the "pre-Pandora" times and the times of the golden
race are similar. Probably Hesiod considered Pandora's story and that of the
golden age as alternatives and, in some ways, not contradictory at all. Yet "pre-
Pandora" times and the times of the golden race could not be considered the
same, since, though similar in quality, they belong to a different "periodization"
of the "beginning" (see Krafft, p. 113). In the same line of interpretation see
J. Fontenrose, "Work, Justice, and Hesiod's Five Ages," *Classical Philology* 69
(1976), especially pp. 2 ff., where the author also demonstrates the kinship of
Hesiod's myth of ages with Indian and Persian myths.

5.   It is, perhaps, curious or strange that a specific reference to "work" (ἔργον)
as a new evil in Pandora's vase does not occur, and that the only mention of
ἔργον applies to the art of weaving in *Erga* 64. Since men had worked even in the
time of the golden race (*Erga* 119)—largely at foodgathering, I assume—Pandora
might not have imported work in itself, but only the painful and compulsory side
of it: fatigue and toil (πόνος). For an emphasis on this point see G. Broccia, "Pandora, il Pithos e la Elpis," *La Parola del Passato*, fasc. 62, vol. 13 (1958): 296 ff.
Yet the text is elusive, or open: ἔργα of *Erga* 64 seems to echo ἀεργόν of *Erga*
44 and therefore to imply that with Pandora the ἔργα are also introduced among

men. This elusiveness is noted by J. Fontenrose, "Work, Justice, and Hesiod's Five Ages," p. 1.

6.   Ἀγκυλομήτης is interpreted by Homer and Hesiod as meaning "with a crooked mind," but the epithet must earlier have meant "with a curved sickle." See Chantraine, *Dict. étym.* and West, *Th.*, p. 158.

7.   The comparison between Prometheus and Perses is somehow confirmed by the careful distinction between Perses' ἁρπάζων and Prometheus's κλέπτειν. For κλέπτειν contains the idea of "deceit" and "dissimulation," while ἁρπάζειν simply means "to rob." This ἁρπάζειν, of course, also connects Perses to the hawk of 203 ff., for the hawk is φέρων (204) the nightingale, while Perses ἄλλα πολλὰ ἐφόρει(ς) (38).

8.   Αὖτις (50). For the meaning, see Kühn, review of *Die "Pandorasage,"* p. 122; Heitsch, "Das Prometheus-Gedicht bei Hesiod," p. 10).

9.   In the *Theogony* the word δῶρον is missing, but there, too, the woman is a gift of Zeus; see 513 and 585 ff.

10.   See, for instance (with κελεύω), *Od.* 6. 198 ff.

11.   A good example in Homer of an *oratio obliqua* is *Il.* 17. 357 ff., where ἀνώγει governs four infinitives. At the end of that command the text continues with ὣς Αἴας ἐπέτελλε πελώριος, a phrase not dissimilar to our ὣς ἔφαθ' (69). A longer indirect order is to be found in *Il.* 9. 680-88, which ends with ὣς ἔφαθ', as in the Hesiodic text. But in these lines of *Iliad* 9 we find three verbs of "saying": ἄνωγεν, ἠπείλησεν, and ἔφη, which make the speaker everpresent in the text and connote the emotional value of his words. In addition, this indirect command is contained in a direct discourse. See also *Il.* 23. 144-49.

12.   One can compare this to at least two passages of Homer where ordering or bidding is equally urgent: *Il.* 15. 146: Ζεὺς σφὼ εἰς Ἴδην κέλετ' ἐλθέμεν ὅττι τάχιστα; and *Od.* 5. 112: τὸν νῦν σ'ἠνώγειν ἀποπεμπέμεν ὅττι τάχιστα.

13.   See *Erga* 108: ὡς ὁμόθεν γεγάασι θεοὶ θνητοί τ' ἄνθρωποι and C. Robert, "Pandora," p. 24, "Denn die erste Weib ist freilich auch wie die ersten Männer, aber nicht von der Erde, sondern aus Erde geformt auf Befehl des Zeus: es ist die Διὸς πλαστὴ γυνή (*Th.* 513)."

14.   Wilamowitz and others took ἐποίησαν to mean "caused men to grow" as, and from the place where, the gods themselves grew ("die Götter lassen die Menschen erwachsen wie und woher sie selbst erwachsen sind") (*Hesiodos Erga*, p. 54). Assumptions like these are often risky, since they furnish a far-fetched remedy. In our text, the verb ἐποίησαν can only mean "created," and Hesiod is obviously struggling with two different stories about the origin of men.

Other scholars think that line 108 does not imply a common birth for men and gods, but simply that the original life of men and gods was equal and common (Sinclair, review of Mazon's trans. of *Hésiode: Théogonie, Les Travaux et les Jours, et le Bouclier, Gnomon* 5 (1929): 627).

Let me add that the version of the creation of men by the gods and by Zeus does not run consistently throughout the myth of the races: when Hesiod comes to the iron race, he fails to specify who its father is. (See Pietro Pucci, "Lévi-Strauss and Classical Culture," *Arethusa* 4 [1971]: 103–17.)

15.   The story of Pandora as a myth about genesis shows the decay of the human race through a series of geneses: the privileged one of males and the subsequent and inferior one of women. Though no explicit reference is made to the male's birth, the text clearly evokes the community of gods and man before Pandora's appearance (*Th.* 535 ff.), and their happy, godlike, natural status (*Erga* 90 ff.). We might therefore deduce that men originated in the same place as the gods, as it is said in line 108.

The myth of the races touches upon the theme of human decay by describing a series of deteriorating races. Indeed, the poet could have portrayed the men of the golden age as born from earth, just as the gods; but, had he done this, he would have left unbalanced the tight parallelism that he sets up among the five races, for a parallel ethical-religious symbolism defines each race in its relationship with the gods. Had the golden race received a birth different from that of the other races, this parallelism would have been impaired.

On the Homeric tradition, see *Il.* 7. 99, where men are formed of earth and water. See M. H. Ninck, "Die Bedeutung des Wasser," *Philol.* Supplem. 14, no. 2 (1921): 28.

16.   From *Il.* 18. 417 ff. we learn of animated golden handmaids molded by Hephaistos, and from *Od.* 7. 91 ff. we learn of his animated golden animals. Thus, it is not surprising that Hermes can animate a creature made of earth; but a molded piece of earth would certainly not be a finished product.

17.   The animated dogs molded by Hephaistos are immortal. (ἀθανάτους ὄντας καὶ ἀγήρως ἤματα πάντα [*Od.* 7. 94], and the golden handmaiden, too, could therefore be immortal.

18.   Krafft, p. 48, n. 2 and p. 105, n. 2 maintains that in Homer and Hesiod, αὐδή does not mean "words" and "language" but "voice" and "sound" of words, and that φωνή, on the contrary, implies "language," "words." This distinction—which is often right and has some support in ancient sources—cannot always be profitably made. For instance, it seems to me arbitrary that in *Od.* 19. 381 Euryclea should recognize Odysseus by the "choice of words" rather than by the "voice"; and, among other passages, see *Th.* 38–40:

> εἴρουσαι . . .
> φωνῇ ὁμηρεῦσαι, τῶν δ' ἀκάματος ῥέει αὐδὴ
> ἐκ στομάτων ἡδεῖα·

with epithets (compare 60 with 70; 63 with 72; 68 with 77-80).

37. Πάνδωρος does not occur in Homer or Hesiod. Its form, as an exocentric nominal compound of the type BAHUVRIHI (see, for instance, περικλῆς, "who has great fame"), suggests the meaning "who possess all gifts" and, therefore, either "fully gifted" or "bounteous." For the latter meaning see Hom. *Epigr.* 7; Bacchyl. frg. 20. 4; Ar. *Aves* 971, etc.

Analogously, πολύδωρος may designate "he who brings many gifts" (see M. I. Finley; "Marriage, Sale and Gift in the Homeric World," *Revue internationale des droits de l'antiquité*, 3d ser., tome 2, 1955, pp. 181 ff. and n. 44), though the old interpretation (Hsch. and Schol. A, *Il.* 6. 394) views πολύδωρος as "he or she who receives [or "costs"] many gifts." Hesiod forces the meaning of the compound by interpreting it as "a gift from all" or "receiving a gift from all."

Regarding the possibility of an intentional pun, let us recall that Hesiod is fond of playing on words. In this passage we have already seen γυιοκόρους μελεδώνας (66) and the probably intentional echoes between περιμήδεα and Προμηθεύς (54) (=*Th.* 510, and see West, *Th.* pp. 308-9), διδασκῆσαι and πολυδαίδαλον (64). Recall Δίκη Διὸς ἐκγεγαυῖα (*Erga* 256), and see *Erga* 6; *Th.* 22.

For a general paper on the problem, see Ernst Risch, "Namensbedeutungen und Worterklärungen bei den ältesten Griechischen Dichtern," *Eumusia: Festgabe für E. Howaldt* (Zürich, 1947), pp. 72 ff. On Hesiod's puns, see Troxler, pp. 8 ff.

38. In this interpretation, πῆμ(α) refers to Pandora of line 81, and the explanation ὅτι . . . ἐδώρησαν is a parenthetical clause.

39. Pl. *Ti.* 48 ff. This third εἶδος is defined both as ὑποδόκη (receptacle) and τιθήνη (nurse), and as πανδεχές (51b) and μητήρ as well.

40. Zeus, too, in his command to the gods, uses the epithet διάκτορος. But there Hermes' role is limited to providing Pandora with a shameless and scheming mind. In the second passage the epithet, as the ancients understood it from ἄγω, suits Hermes' πομπή of Pandora.

41. The textual phrase "something similar to a modest virgin" preserves the idea of Pandora as a copy and imitation of something else. Our translation places the emphasis on the neuter ἴκελον (71), thereby stressing the abstractness of the copy and the difference of the copy from the models. The phrase παρθένῳ αἰδοίη ἴκελον covers the same part of the line as *Il.* 5. 450: αὐτῷ τ' Αἰνεία ἴκελον. See also *Il.* 24. 80.

42. Whether or not by "modest virgin" we should understand a goddess— as in Zeus's command—remains an open question. Certainly, it would be possible to extrapolate logically from the text that Hephaistos has no other possible model but that of a goddess and to imply that Κρονίδεω διὰ βουλάς (71) states

Hephaistos's obedience to Zeus's precise order. On the other hand, the text
could also be read as ironical, viz., as purposely stressing Hephaistos's obedience
even as he disobeys, and the phrase of 71 could simply mean "something like
a virgin today." In my opinion, both the heavy logical implication of the first
reading and the unjustified irony of the second should be avoided. The text
preserves the idea of imitation, while the emphasis on the divine model is no
longer there.

The difficulty we meet at this point clearly shows the shortcoming of a
formal philological analysis. Given the two passages cited below, no philological analysis would resolve the question that we are asking.

$$\mathit{ἀθανάτης\ δὲ\ θεῆς\ εἰς\ ὦπα\ ἐίσκειν}$$
$$\mathit{παρθενικῆς\ καλὸν\ εἶδος\ ἐπήρατον·}$$
$$(Erga\ 62\text{-}63)$$
$$\mathit{παρθένῳ\ αἰδοίῃ\ ἴκελον\ Κρονίδεω\ διὰ\ βουλάς}$$
$$(Erga\ 71)$$

For no contradictions occur between the two passages, and Κρονίδεω διὰ
βουλάς would take into account all variations.

43.   Both expressions (ζῶσε, κόσμησε [72]) are Homeric, though κοσμέω
refers habitually to good order in military ranks, in preparing meals, and in
arranging the house. But κόσμος in the sense of "dressing up," or "toilette,"
is *hapax* in *Il.* 14. 187. For the difference between *Erga* 72 and *Th.* 573 ff.,
see Krafft, p. 102.

44.   Some scholars agree with Robert in thinking that Athena first weaves or
has someone weave Pandora's dress and, therefore, by teaching the craft to Pandora, obeys her father's command. Only subsequently does she have Pandora
dressed. This interpretation can be defended if one presses the logical steps of
Athena's action and if one underlines the subordination of this text to Zeus's
command. But even if the craft and the teaching of the craft are somehow
present in the back of the reader's mind, the text does not mention them.

45.   Here again the contradiction emerges as a direct result of Hesiod's paradoxical representation of Pandora. In order to represent her total negativity,
the text interprets her as a gift bane of the gods, but in order to be coherent
with the themes of Pandora as first woman and Pandora's beauty, the text
connects her with the pleasant floral symbolism.

46.   The entire passage

$$\mathit{πρῶτος\ γάρ\ ῥα\ Διὸς\ πλαστὴν\ ὑπέδεκτο\ γυναῖκα}$$
$$\mathit{παρθένον}$$
$$(Th.\ 513\text{-}15)$$

is difficult, and its meaning has been debated. It is generally understood to
mean "Epimetheus first accepted the molded virgin of Zeus as his wife."
The genitive would then imply origin or paternity.

47.   *Erga* 57 (=*Th.* 570): "In place of fire (ἀντὶ πυρός) I'll give a bane. . . ."
For an analysis of this expression, see pp. 95 ff.

48.   While all the MSS transmit line 99, Plutarch, Stobaeus, and Origen do
not quote it, and the Scholia Vetera do not comment on it. Of these *testimonia*,
Stobaeus cannot be considered a proof, since he quotes only 96-98 about Elpis,
disregarding Pandora's action in lifting the lid and, of course, that of shutting
it again. He either recasts the passage or he quotes by heart, for he makes
πῶμα the subject of line 98 and interprets it "Hope did not flee, for the lid
stopped her [Stobaeus reads ἐπέλλαβε and adds an unmetrical μιν] ." Of the
other two *testimonia*, Plutarch provides the more serious evidence against
line 99 (Origen is often careless). For, though Plutarch is capable of athetizing for moralistic reasons (for instance, he condemns *Erga* 267-73: see
Scholia Vetera, ed. Pertusi), the fact that the *Scholia* report Plutarch's athe-
tization of *Erga* 267-73 and not that of *Erga* 99 leaves room for doubt. If the
line received Plutarch's moral censure, as is possible, we should probably expect an analogous note on the part of the scholiast. But how decisive can the
silence of the scholiast on this point be? In modern criticism the moral un-
easiness might still be detected. Wilamowitz (p. 53) for instance, asks what
Zeus wished to do by setting the evil in the *pithos*. "He could send it to men
without this detour." Wilamowitz, then, lets himself be guided by his experience of the truly naive tales when he adds: "An end such as 'Fortunately the
lid fell before Hope got out,' befits such naive stories." While the weight of
the tradition does not constitute any serious proof against 99, it is possible
that subjective reasons dictate the old and the new athetizations. But then the
philologist, expert in naive tales, must rewrite the episode itself; thus Wilamowitz invents the story that Pandora is frightened ("erschreckte") and lets the
lid fall unintentionally. This is indeed a story in the style of Grimm.

   A formal argument against the line, grounded on the double epithet in the
line, does not appear too serious when one compares it to lines 1, 8, 18, etc.

49.   See Solmsen, p. 81: "For, granted that the evils are powerful and that
they were brought into this world by Night, there remains the question,'What
is their place in a world order which not Night, but Zeus, controls?' The poet
of the *Works and Days* wonders why and under what conditions Zeus allows
the evils to hold sway." In this passage Solmsen is rightly aware of the fact
that "contradictions must not always be denied, expelled or explained away,
but they may be indicative either of the complexity of the subject or of the
intensity of the poet's struggle with it."

50.   Krafft, pp. 108 ff., presents the ingenious and suggestive interpretation
that Pandora, by lifting the lid of the *pithos*, spreads and disperses all the
means of livelihood. The spontaneously created provisions having been lost,
man must then work. Krafft's argument is well elaborated, but the odds are

against it. To illustrate some of the difficulties: Krafft must interpret Elpis as a good entity. But in order to do so he must understand line 100, ἄλλα δέ μυρία λυγρά ("other innumerable evils [besides Elpis] roam about"), in an improbable way; i.e., "dafür ist aber Anderes, unzählige Übel über sie gekommen" (p. 111). This meaning is most unlikely, even granting the absence of the article; see *Il.* 9. 365, etc., where the same absence does not imply a predicative meaning of ἄλλα.

Moreover, Krafft is forced to explain the origin of the evils that roam the world as a direct result of the disappearance of man's livelihood. Toil, poverty, hunger would thus be explained, but what about νοῦσοι, "diseases"? Krafft takes νοῦσος in the vague sense in which it is used in *Od.* 15. 407 ff. Yet Hesiod does not seem to have the Homeric passage in mind: for one thing, he does not mention want, πενίη–which is coupled with νοῦσος in *Od.* 15. 407 ff.–and uses the word νοῦσος twice in the plural (93 and 101). Furthermore, in line 92 (νούσων τ'ἀργαλέων, αἴ τ'ανδράσι κῆρας ἔδωκαν) the epithet ἀργαλέων recalls *Il.* 13. 667, where the word means sickness and has nothing to do with hunger. Finally the relative clause, αἴ . . ., etc., would naturally imply violent diseases [κῆρας being accepted by eds.].

For the evils contained in the jar, see Solmsen, p. 83, n. 23.

51.   Ἐλπίς properly means a larger set of expectations or anticipations than our "hope," for it implies hope, expectation, and even fear, as in Homer *Il.* 13. 309; 17. 239, etc.

52.   κενεὴν ἐπὶ ἐλπίδα μίμνων (498) can be understood in various ways. (a) With ἐπί governing ἐλπίδα, we might understand (1) "in view of," or "for the purpose of a vain elpis;" or (2) "near," "by vain Elpis." (For a pregnant sense of ἐπί plus the accusative see LSJ ἐπί C.I. 2.)
(b) With ἐπί in tmesis with μίμνω: "Awaiting vain elpis." This last interpretation is the least probable, since ἐπιμίμνω plus the accusative is very rare and the idea of "waiting for elpis" is a confused notion, especially in view of line 500 where Elpis accompanies (κομίζει) man.

53.   κακὰ προσελέξατο θυμῷ (499) is difficult, and it is interpreted either as "to speak to oneself" or "to gather for himself."

54.   In *Od.* 18. 328-29 λέσχη seems to be a place in which people would sleep, similar to the smithy, but different from it:

οὐδ ἐθέλεις εὕδειν χαλκήϊον ἐς δόμον ἐλθὼν
ἠέ που ἐς λέσχην
nor do you feel like going to sleep in the smithy or
in the lounge.

But in *Erga* 493 ff.

πὰρ δ'ἴθι χάλκειον θῶκον καὶ ἐπαλέα λέσχην
ὥρῃ χειμερίῃ ὁπότε κρύος ἀνέρας ἔργων
ἰσχάνει

λέσχη must be a place of idleness and chatter, as the entire semantic development of the word implies. Mazon translated it "parloir de la ville." The connection between Elpis and the man deprived of βίος has been forcefully made by G. Broccia in "Pandora, il Pithos e la Elpis," pp. 302 ff. He is certainly right in emphasizing that the advent of Pandora goes along with Zeus's hiding of the livelihood.

55. ἐπαλέα λέσχην (493): ἐπαλέα from ἐπαλής is variously understood by commentators. Chantraine, *Dict. étym.*, s.v. ἐπαλής, defends the meaning "sunny," which is the traditional meaning of the old commentators, and translates the Hesiodean phrase with "le portique ensoleillé." In this case the ἐπαλέα λέσχην could be a different place from the smithy, in accordance with *Od.* 18. 328-29 where the smithy and the λέσχη are introduced by the disjunctive particle, ἠέ.

Others take ἐπαλής to mean "crowded"; see, for instance, E. Boisacq, *Dictionnaire étymologique de la langue Grecque*, 4th ed. (Heidelberg, 1950), s.v. ἐπαλής; Sinclair agrees with this meaning and writes (p. 54) that the smithy "is not a separate place from ἐπαλέα λέσχην. The λέσχη was part of the smithy."

56. Many interpreters do not accept the idea of Elpis as available for a good cause. The captivity of Elpis in the jar is, of course, an old riddle of our text, for, if Elpis is kept prisoner, as a kakon, how can we meet Elpis later in the text and, presumably, even as a good discourse? Lesky, Fink, and others have suggested that here Hesiod confuses two themes. On the one hand, there is the story of a jar containing all good things: what is inside belongs to the owner of the vase, and what leaves the vase is lost to him. On the other hand, the same story depicts a jar containing evils: kept inside, the evils do not exist for men, but if they are allowed to fly out they spread to men.

57. For γονεῦσιν (*Erga* 235) = fathers, see Chantraine, *Dict. étym.*, s.v. γίγνομαι. On the likeness of children to parents, and in particular to the father, cf. *Od.* 1. 208-9; 4. 141, etc.; Eur. *Heraclidae* 509-14, 540-41; Lucr. 1. 597-98; 4. 1218-24; Livy. 10.7.3: *"rettulisse dicitur Decius parentis sui speciem"*; Verg. *Aen.* 4. 329: *qui te tamen ore referret; Aen.* 7. 49; 12. 348: *"nomine avum referens, animo manibusque parentem"*; *Aen.* 6. 768: *"qui te nomine reddet"*; 4. 84: *"genitoris imagine."*

58. The χηρωσταί are collateral or contractual relatives. See Eust. 533. 30 and Detienne, *Crise agraire*, p. 16, n. 12.

59. Σύμφορος here takes its meaning from the verb συμφέρω or συμφέρομαι in the sense of "to agree with, to comply with, to live, be in harmony with": Ar. *Lys.* 166; Eur. *Med.* 13. Hesychius, very properly, interprets a similar instance of σύμφορος in *Erga* 302 as συμπίπτων καὶ συνών, i.e., "agreeing and living together" as a companion or as a lover. In the text of *Th.* 593 the idea of "lover" may not be too far off, especially since συμφέρεσθαι is said of

amorous agreement between men and women, as in the quoted passages, and even of sexual intercourse.

60.   Πυγοστόλος is variously understood by interpreters. See Sinclair, p. 40 and Troxler, p. 160.

61.   For the woman as a watcher of what is inside, see Xen. *Oec.* 7. 18: τοῦ σώσαντος ταῦτα. According to Ps. Arist. *Oec.* 1344a 1 ff. it is true to women's physis to preserve what is inside: τὸ δὲ σώζῃ τὰ ἔνδον.

62.   I understand "another son" to mean "a grandson." Rzach and other editors prefer Hermann's correction (θάνοι) to the MSS' θάνοις and supply the subject from μουνογενής: "and he [viz., your son] may die late leaving another son."

Others, Mazon and Colonna, for example, leave the text as it stands, and they interpret ἕτερον as "in your place."

On the economic importance of Hesiod's precept in this time of agricultural crisis, see Detienne, *Crise agraire*, pp. 15 ff.

63.   Φέρβειν occurs first in *Erga* 377.

64.   In *Il.* 24. 540-41, Achilles speaks of the duty of the son toward the parents and of the expectations of the parents by the son. He regrets not having taken care of his old father (οὐδέ νυ τόν γε γεράσκοντα κομίζω). This duty was, of course, a familiar principle in ancient Greece.

On the immortality provided by the woman through procreation, see Arist. *De An. Gen.* 2. 1. 731b, 32 ff; *De Anima* 2. 4. 415a, 26-30 etc. See also Ps. Arist., *Oec.* 1243b 24 ff.: "At the same time, nature by cycle [parents and children] obtains an everlasting life (τὸ ἀεὶ εἶναι) since it cannot preserve life in relation to the individual, but in relation to the species (κατὰ τὸ εἶδος)."

65.   Arist. *Oec.* 1344a 15 ff. approvingly quotes the precept of Hesiod, adding that "difference of habits is least conducive to affection (αἱ γὰρ ἀνομοιότητες τῶν ἠθῶν ἥκιστα φιλικόν)." The woman must, therefore, learn man's ways. This is a point on which Medea comments bitterly (Eur. *Med.* 238-40). See also Xenoph. *Oec.* 7. 5 ff.; and Arist. *Pol.* 1. 13. 1260b, 15-16.

66.   Here and elsewhere I have used the metaphor "matrix of oppositions" to indicate that the oppositions arise and are at once displaced in the wake of the difference, but the difference cannot be thought of as another metaphysical "origin." See J. Derrida, *De la grammatologie* (Paris, 1967).

Chapter 5
CONCLUSIONS:
AGRICULTURE, TRADE, DISCORD, AND POETRY

For the changes of everything awake man's
intelligence and prevent his rest.
Hippocrates, *De aeris, aquis locis*

Having briefly touched upon the relationship that underlies justice and
agriculture in Hesiod's text, we must now attempt to ascertain whether this
ideological link makes Hesiod partial to or hostile toward trade and crafts. The
question has special relevance because all that we know of Hesiod suggests that
he did not approve of the way the basileis used their power, and because his
age is marked by many signs of crises. One might, therefore, anticipate that Hesiod
would favor the new ways of production that were emerging in his time and beginning to shake the old political and social structure.

The *Erga*, indeed, provides historians with enough material to enable them
to speak of an agricultural crisis in Hesiod's time.[1] The evidence for this crisis
may be found in the following facts:
1) The collective ownership of the *genos* has begun to disintegrate, as is evident
from Hesiod's and Perses' division of their father's farm.
2) Land appears to be alienable by sale: the pressure of this alienation already
threatens the small farmers (*Erga* 341).[2]
3) The economic process is no longer limited to agriculture, piracy, and crafts.
Trade has gained momentum, as is evident from various facts. Hesiod's father
himself was a merchant (πλωΐζεσκ' ἐν νηυσί [*Erga* 633 ff.]), combining this
activity with farming in order to acquire some wealth: βίου κεχρημένος
ἐσθλοῦ (*Erga* 634). Hesiod's advice to his brother Perses to imitate their father
and to trade during the months of August and September implies that trade
can channel the surplus from farming and crafts. Another hint in the text confirms the impression that trading activity was on the increase in Hesiod's time:
in the *Erga* the word ἐμπορίη (trade) occurs for the first time.[3]

Though it is impossible to say how widespread trade was in this era, it is
certainly plausible to assume some use of monetary equivalents like iron and

gold bars. This must be true, in spite of the fact that while in Homer we find the word τάλαντον and even ἡμιτάλαντον, there is no mention of money in Hesiod.[4]

The activity of trade, by providing an open market, must also have encouraged professional competition among farmers and craftsmen. We are therefore not surprised to find praise of this competition in the opening lines of the *Erga* (11-24).[5]

Contrary to a somewhat traditional view, which considers Hesiod to be the representative of poor peasants and farmers, I would agree with the view that Hesiod speaks as a farmer who is possessed of some capital and who strives for wealth. The farmer he speaks of not only possesses his house, barn, and farm, but he also owns his cattle (436-40) and has a serving girl (602-3), with other servants probably available for special occasions (502, 573, 597, etc.). He also possesses a large boat (624 ff.) on which he can load the surplus of his produce or someone else's (although this last possibility is not mentioned).

Hesiod shows some personal qualms, or at least ambivalence, about trade. On the one hand, he encourages the accumulation of wealth by trading, but on the other, he recognizes the risks of such activity (*Erga* 689 ff.), given the imprudent greed of men (*Erga* 682-86); and he confesses that he has never sailed for trade (*Erga* 649 ff.) This ambiguity does not prevent Hesiod from speaking in favor of an activity already engaged in by his father, especially if it be undertaken with proper caution.

Trade, like plowing, was introduced among men when Zeus hid man's livelihood (*Erga* 42-46). Two steps are implied in the process by which trade restores what has been lost: (1) farming or crafts must produce goods in excess of immediate needs, and (2) these goods must be removed from their protected place in the house and transported to places where they do not exist or are scarce. The goods may return to the house in larger quantity, but only after a dangerous displacement. Hesiod is particularly sensitive to this danger, and his attitude toward it is ambiguous. He recommends putting all the freight on the ship in the good season (672); but a few lines later, speaking of the dangerous spring sailing, he warns Perses:

> Do not put all your livelihood in hollow ships,
> but leave the greater part and put on board the
> lesser.

This cautious advice (see also 694) contradicts the very goal of trade, making great gains, as the poet implies at line 672 and explicitly announces in 643-45:

> Praise the small ship, but put your goods
> (φορτία) in a large one. The greater the

cargo, the greater the gain upon gain will be if
the winds withhold evil blasts.

The precious livelihood, so patiently and laboriously stored in the house to be present and at hand, must be removed, must become absent and deferred, in order to be re-stored again in larger quantity in the house. This movement of transformation is well expressed in the language of the text. What is present (τὸ παρέον [366], τὸ κατακείμενον [364]) must become cargo (φορτία, φόρτος [644, 690]); viz., it must become "something carried away."[6] The restoration of the goods is achieved, therefore, after removing the goods from the house and embarking them on a dangerous trip under the sign of destruction and death (687, 691).

These texts show that trade and navigation imply a movement that contradicts the goal of Hesiod's utopia. For confirmation we need only turn to *Erga* 45 and 236-37: men did not sail either before the coming of Pandora or in the dreamed City of Justice.

Explicit mention of craft or "manufacturing" is found only in Hesiod's praise of good competition (*Erga* 20 ff.); it is, therefore, impossible to say anything about craft itself. Nevertheless, it is possible to see that Hesiod's perplexity about trade and, as we will see, his treatment of competition in the marketplace are at odds with his ideal mode of production, farming. Farming discloses and recovers the gift of Earth that the advent of Pandora has hidden; it therefore confirms the existence of an "original" *locus* of divine assistance in a movement not unlike that of poetry, which recovers the "original" *locus* of truth hidden by the deceitful imitation initiated by Pandora.

Trade and craft do not possess the immediacy of the divine presence; on the contrary, they forever hide the "original" *locus* and the "original" gifts. Trade displaces goods, and the products of "technology" (in the competition of the market) involve a process of imitation in which the others, not truth, are models.

Notwithstanding the tentative praise of navigation, trade, and competition in the market, Hesiod's real alliance remains with the farmers, not necessarily because of a political and ideological community with the old world, but because of the strategy of his metaphysics. His advice is to desert the agora—the place where commercial dealings take place—for it is a place of contention: Dikê, we recall, is dragged captive into the marketplace. The agora will, however, be the center of struggles for the sake of a new dikê in the *polis*, and for the sake of a new political life.

Although Hesiod seems to favor the modes of production whose social and economic development will eliminate the old order, his text denies such sympathy by evoking an elegiac utopia.

It would, however, be wrong not to emphasize the power of subversion that the praise of Discord in economic competition elicits in Hesiod's text. In *Theogony* 226 ff. Hesiod had represented Eris (Discord) as the daughter of the Night, entirely evil, mother of murderous children. This negative representation is obviously in agreement with the rest of Hesiod's metaphysical gesture toward identity and presence. For Discord, by definition, denies the identity and, by implying an endless detour of rivalry and struggles, forever removes the presence of the fixed *locus* of truth and plenty. Discord therefore carries within herself the negative implications of difference and deferral; Discord is, in fact, one possible name for such movement.

In the *Erga* Hesiod develops a new view of Discord: with an emphatic tone of recantation, the poet, immediately after the proem, asserts that two kinds of Discord exist, one evil and one good (11). The evil Discord, cruel as it is, is blameworthy and hated by men since it excites war and battles, while the other Discord promotes professional competition:

> She [Competition] stirs even the helpless
> (ἀπάλαμον) to work. For one who
> needs to work, seeing another man (ἕτερον)
> who is rich, hastens to plow, and to plant, and
> to set his house in good order.[7] And neighbor
> competes with neighbor, hastening to be rich. This
> Eris is good to men. And the potter is resentful
> of the potter, the carpenter of the carpenter,
> the beggar is jealous of the beggar, the poet
> of the poet.
>   (20 ff.)

We confront here a dichotomy analogous to that which we have seen drawn in the case of the wife. The highly ambivalent nature of Discord creates an equally precarious distinction between what is good and what is bad.

The boldness of Hesiod's new interpretation of Discord must be explained: he wants some characteristics of Discord to be ranked with the positive terms—Muses, Dikê, etc.—that insure the achievement of plenty, truth, and identity. Simultaneously he justifies the rivalry of poets and gives a favorable interpretation to economic competition in the marketplace.

Accordingly, Hesiod draws a neat line of demarcation between the two daughters of Night. The evil one is younger, and this fact might suggest that her birth occurred after, or at the time of, the decay of the world. "No man loves" evil Discord, says Hesiod (15), but good Discord is "much better" (πολλὸν ἀμείνω [19]) for mortals.[8]

In accordance with this distinction and separation, Discord is appropriated by Hesiod as a positive power. This point is important because it shows clearly the poet's way of thinking: threatening powers do exist, but men should try to escape the influence of such negative powers. Accordingly, for Hesiod the line between positive and negative forces marks an ethical decision: only when he ranks Discord among the good powers does he praise it as something that men should follow and accept.

But it is possible to see that the line drawn by Hesiod does not separate anything: just as the *limen* of the house is always transgressed by women, so the separation of the two kinds of Discord remains a wish. Indeed the two kinds of discord not only have the same name and genealogy, but they are both inevitable. The bad Eris is imposed by Necessity, and the good one is "set by Zeus in the roots of the Earth." Both excite violent rivalry: the ζῆλος provoked by the good Eris indicates a violent, hateful envy (see *Erga* 192)[9] and in other contexts κότος often defines the feelings that precede a real fight (*Aspis* 176, 803).

Finally, these two kinds of Eris are inseparable not only in real economic relations (Welskopf, p. 127) but even within Hesiod's text. When Hesiod abuses the other poets, saying with the Muses; "Shepherds of the fields, poor fools, mere bellies" (*Th.* 26), we cannot be sure whether he is competing peacefully or waging a scathing attack, but we are certain that Hesiod's rivals will not "love" this attack.

As the boundary line between the two kinds of Eris becomes blurred, Eris will work with all her destructive and productive power. At this junction we might recall the murderous, hateful children of Eris (*Th.* 266 ff.) and imagine their intervention in the contest excited by Eris.

Yet we do not need to imagine the blood and the strife that Discord and her children (Toil, Forgetfulness, Hunger, Grief, Fights, Battles, Murders, Lies, Discourses, and Disputes) spread: it is sufficient to see how even the good Discord pushes man outside himself to gape enviously and angrily at other men; it forces a man to imitate others and to make his life a perpetual search for wealth (an evil goal: see *Erga* 686) in an endless detour and protraction of his aims. Similarly, even the good Discord must imply a confused demarcation between the self and the other—like the crooked line of the plowman who gapes intensely at others.

Hesiod, therefore, fails to tame Discord and to channel her power toward the achievement of a peaceful fullness and presence. He fails because the letter of his text does not obey the metaphysical constriction he has imposed on the text. Discord locates itself in his text, in his language, in the form of an irresolvable tension. Discord vibrates as that force of instability and precariousness that prevents the text from being fully consistent and leaves an indisposable excess of meaning.[10] Accordingly, the very description of the good Eris itself contains its own disintegration. Conversely, the evil Eris will not be a barrier to the positive aspects of the good Eris. As a result, the polarity "evil Eris : good Eris" becomes an empty form. Each pole of this polarity, instead of remaining at its fixed position, "drifts," so to speak, from its place; or, by containing its own disintegration, it fails to act as a pole, as an opposition. Some inner excess precludes the possibility of the opposition.

The consequence of this argument is that the Hesiodic polarities only *formally* function as the conceptual frame that embraces a whole phenomenon.[11] In reality, since the two poles fail to remain fixed at the extreme points of the axis, the polarity Competition (a): Discord (b) turns into a chiastic structure. At one pole, *a* also reveals *b*, and at the other pole *b* also reveals *a*.

In view of this thorough ambivalence, the problem of interpretation becomes difficult: should we ally ourselves with Hesiod's confidence that the phenomenon of Discord can be channeled toward a presence, or should we simply recognize that the goal is not sustained by his text?

If we come to the latter conclusion we must assess and describe in full the force that struggles with Hesiod's metaphysical construction, the excess of meaning that prevents his text from being consistent within itself. In both cases, we face an impossible question, namely, how do we as readers interpret an intention distinguished by the text that simultaneously gives the text its energy to proceed and contradicts it?

Before we investigate these problems more deeply, we should review the other myths and narratives in which we have identified patterns similar to the one found in the text about Discord. In other instances examined we have found a similar dichotomy or polarization, and a similar instability or precariousness in that polarity.

We may recall the myth of poetry, so crucial to Hesiod's metaphysics, the tenets of which spread so deeply through his text. In this myth we see the poet as the provider of divine gifts: a straight *logos* of truth pitted against a falsely truthful one, a sweet balm, sung by the poet after his initiation by the Muses, which turns men away from their griefs. Yet behind this facade we have read in the same text that these gifts, by insinuating a dangerous oblivion of the self, may turn into poison; and, far from being sweet, they strike violently against other poets. Moreover, the literal emphasis on the deflecting and persuasive words of basileis and poets subverts the straightness of their discourse; this, in turn, casts serious doubt on their truth; i.e., on their straight mirroring of things as they are. The myth of poetry therefore gazes on presence, while the letter of the myth bespeaks absence in addition. The line that divides presence and absence passes through imitation: only the Muses can draw that line, for they are masters of both the distorting imitation and the perfect one.

Here again, as in the case of Eris, the pole constituted by the discourse of truth already contains in itself the menace of its own disintegration; the explicit polarities "truthful discourse : simulated truthful discourse" and "straight : crooked," etc., therefore become empty forms. No axis connects *and* separates the two poles; no distance keeps the truthful discourse in a safe place.

The collapse of the polarized structure uncovers a chiastic figure: we may schematize this figure as *a b, b a*. One pole, *a*, that of truth, straightness, and sweetness, reveals, under the surface of the text, the movement of crookedness, deceit, and violence (*b*); and accordingly the opposite pole, that of deceit, violence, oblivion (*b*) also reveals the movement of *a*.[12]

But the story of the myth of poetry is not finished. At the beginning of the *Erga*, in a totally different context, we find the praise of poetic competition, and in another passage (*Erga* 650 ff.) we hear the poet describing his voyage to a poetic contest, at the funeral games of Amphidamas. Here he wins the first prize, a tripod, which he in turn offers to the Muses who taught him his song.[13]

The poet, then, knows that he sings in a climate of rivalry and jealousy. In the *ainos* that he tells to the basileis he reveals that he sings under the burden of violence. The subversive power of Discord that jeopardizes the elegiac meaning of the myth finds explicit recognition here. But the text is not content with this realistic assertion of violence and toil. Tracing a utopian line, Hesiod goes on to assure that the good Discord is productive, loved by men, competitive but not violent: such reassurances evoke again the sweet gift of the Muses. The Muses' truthful imitation and the good imitation prodded by the positive Eris move toward the same goal.

Nevertheless, the line drawn by Hesiod fails to make a neat separation of the two Erises: accordingly, the text reveals the chiastic figure we have already described. The chiastic figures uncovered in the myths of the Muses and of Eris combine perfectly and support one another.

The same movement can be detected in the myth of Pandora and in Hesiod's precepts concerning wives. Pandora is pitted against the world of identity, plenty, and presence, and therefore occupies the pole of absence, scarcity, and deceitful imitation. By arriving in the world she removes the world of presence in an act of imitation of presence. Because of this very act of imitation, we have argued, she cannot legitimately occupy the negative pole. On the contrary, she blurs all distinctions: since Zeus himself cooperates with her in destroying human happiness, the space that divides Pandora from her opposite values, as deep as that which now divides gods and men, is easily bridged.

Mindful of the characteristics of Pandora, Hesiod abuses the woman as a destroyer of the house, of man's happiness, of his goods. But since the *limen* of the house is not a sufficient barrier against her, Hesiod urges the husband to appropriate woman and teach her his ways. This effort at taming the upsetting qualities of woman is never totally successful because of her tricky and unconquerable nature. Invariably we arrive at the same conclusion: a sort of chiastic figure replaces the polarity and introduces a strained, inverted arrangement. The terms are arranged in an inverted order (*a b b a*), and because of their repetition, these terms open a tautological yet inverted movement.[14]

Though Hesiod's text is sustained by clear and tight polarities, we have uncovered a structure—the chiastic one—that in fact dissolves the polarities into paradoxes, i.e., into tautologies marked by an inverted rhetorical emphasis. Yet the explicit polarization may explain why the precariousness of the metaphysical construction remained hidden from the classical culture. Granted that Hesiod appears as the religious teacher of the Greeks, that his poetic mission is felt as a religious mission, that he speaks in the name of truth and justice; the question remains, "How does his text react to these metaphysical solicitations?"

Our analysis has shown that the voice of Hesiod, in becoming the voice of Dikè, of the Muses, of good Eris, simultaneously assumes discordant notes that reveal the force and the violence of its aim. The metaphysical tradition's blindness to this discordance, to the inverted and paradoxical movement that prevents the polar movement from closing up, testifies to the force of this metaphysics.

We must, instead, recognize the energy and the force that jeopardize Hesiod's project, and focus on the movement of this force in Hesiod's text. Three of the narratives we have analyzed, the myths of poetry, of Pandora, and of Eris, concern three forms or strategies of imitation: language as imitation of things as they are, culture as imitation of nature, and competition as imitation of the other.

Hesiod presents solutions that have a long history in Western thought,[15] but it is more important here to emphasize the difficulty and ambiguity of the notion of imitation and the excess it implies. For imitation suggests an additional element, i.e., the copy as distinguished from the model, the representation as *simulacrum* of the model; and accordingly the distance from and the difference between the representation and the model. It is, therefore, evidence of extraordinary coherence that Hesiod is able to wage such a battle against the corrupting and supplementary power of imitation. He tries to reduce this excess either by denying its existence (for example, when he assumes the possibility of a discourse that imitates things as they are *perfectly*,) or by ranking it among the evils that men should try to avoid or be able to control.

In this connection Hesiod's praise of Discord represents his most daring gesture, for notwithstanding the dichotomy he introduces between two kinds of Discords ("they have opposite minds" [*Erga* 13]), their contiguity remains an inevitable element of threat. Even the bland kind of Discord is implanted by

Zeus "in the roots of Earth" and therefore appears inevitable. But, as our analysis has shown, the two divine powers act in concert: their force penetrates the most sacred images of Hesiod's metaphysics, infusing violence and contention in the sweet and appeasing song of the Muses, arming the weak victim of injustice with the bravery of a fighter, or sustaining an opposition between farming and economic competition. Accordingly, this power carries with itself not only the hope of truth and victory but also the menace of defeat, of scorn, and death in the battle in which everything is wagered.

This description of Discord's activity, however, is only a thematic outline of the presence of this divine power in Hesiod's text. More profound is the effect of Discord in the constitution of the text, as the force that combines two opposite minds, that constitutes another figure of imitation, difference, and detour, forever removing the text from presence while always pushing toward it. Then we see that Discord sits in the middle of the polarities so carefully drawn, holding the opposite terms together in an upsetting tension that no metaphysical polarization can tame, but only disguise. Accordingly, the text shows that only by disguising the nature of Discord are the metaphysical polarities made possible, and that only in the act of separating the two minds of Discord are the metaphysical reassurances attained. Yet to separate the two minds of Discord is to deny discord itself, just as to imply identity in imitation is to contradict the notion of imitation. Thus Discord holds the text in a grip that is both creative and ruinous, impressing on it a rhythmical imbalance of moves that imperils its construction; she thus endangers a text made possible by her actions but designed to resist and imprison her.

NOTES

1.   Among the most recent publications, see M. Detienne, *Crise agraire et attitude religieuse chez Hésiode*, Collection "Latomus" 68 (Brussels-Berchem, 1963); C. G. Starr, *The Origin of the Greek Civilization* (New York, 1961).
2.   On the alienation of land by sale see D. Asheri, "Laws of Inheritance, Distribution of Land, and Political Constitution in Ancient Greece," *Historia* 12 (1963): 1 ff.
3.   H. Knorringa, *Emporos*, 1961[2], pp. 4-5.
4.   On the use of metals and metal bars before the invention of coins, see, for instance: G. de Sanctis, *Storia dei Greci* 1, 453-59; P. Wade-Gery, *Perachora* 1, 187-89.

5.   E. C. Welskopf, *Probleme der Musse im alten Hellas* (Berlin, 1962), p. 127,
shows how Hesiod wishes to separate good from evil competition, though in
real economic relations the two forms are inseparable.

On the striking novelty of production for the market, see J. H. Hasebroek,
Griechische Wirtschaft-und Gesellschaftsgeschichte (Tübingen, 1931). On the
emergence of the individual, see, among the most recent publications, M. I.
Finley, *Early Greece: The Bronze and the Archaic Ages* (London, 1970).
6.   Φόρτος, φορτίον, and φορτίζω are found only in the *Erga*, the last two
for the first time in Greek literature. Φόρτος is found twice in Homer: *Od.* 8.
163; 14. 296.
7.   Depending on how one reads the text, the meaning could also be: "For
one becomes eager for work when one looks at another, a rich man, who is
hastening to plow. . . ." For a recent and accurate discussion of the passage, see
Bona Quaglia, p. 39, n. 11. She translates as I do in this note.
8.   The difference between the two kinds of Eris is then made rhetorically
explicit by the use of the epithets. Πόλεμον κακόν (14), σχετλίη (15), and
βαρεῖαν (16) are pitted against ἀμείνω (19) and ἀγαθή (24).
9.   Ζῆλος and ζηλόω are found for the first time in Hesiod. Φθονέω is
hapax in Hesiod, while the noun φθόνος does not occur either in Homer or
in Hesiod.

For ζῆλος and φθόνος in the sense of "literary imitation," see G. Pasquali,
Orazio Lirico (Florence, 1964), pp. 119 ff.
10.   This metaphor needs to be explained: by this expression we indicate that
excess which comes about from the polysemy of the text. For instance, in line
11 Hesiod says that Eris is not of one γένος: we can interpret the word either
as "kind" or "race." However, we realize that the "race" of the two sisters is
the same: both are daughters of Night (*Th.* 224-25; *Erga* 17). Thus, oddly
enough, the poet tells us that Eris is not of one γένος and then he gives us the
γένος of good Eris as identical to that of evil Eris. In this instance, the word
γένος produces an excess of meaning. We have shown that Hesiod's text presents countless similar instances in which the meaning, so to speak, is unstable
and drifts away.
11.   On the "polarity" as the mode of Hesiod's myth and a mode of Greek
thought, see P. Philippson, "Genealogie als mythische Form" in *Hesiod*,
Herausgegeben von E. Heitsch (Darmstadt, 1966), pp. 685 ff. The author
outlines the peculiar polarity of Hesiod's myths as the combination of "zwei
polare Gegensätzlichkeiten die als solche zusammen eine Totalität bilden"
(p. 685). She distinguishes this Greek form of polarity from the form typical
of monistic or dualistic modes of thinking (Denkform): in the latter case the
polar terms exclude each other or annihilate each other in conflict, or, becoming reconciled, are lifted and conserved as oppositions (sich versöhnend

als Gegensätze aufheben" (p. 686). In the Hesiodic polarity, on the contrary, the poles are not separable, but are determined in their conceptual, polar existence by the opposition itself.

Phillippson considers the Hesiodic polarity as a form that embraces a whole phenomenon: but she fails to see that the opposite terms "drift," as we have shown, and that the polarity becomes an empty frame. Furthermore, the author seems to neglect the boundary line that Hesiod draws between opposite terms. Surely the line fails to separate the opposite terms, but the act of drawing it suggests Hesiod's ethical point of view and also a tendency toward the dualistic mode of thinking.

On polarity in Greek speculative thought see G. E. R. Lloyd, *Polarity and Analogy* (Cambridge, 1966).

12.   The term *chiasmus* in this sense is modern (see H. Lansberg, *Handbuch der Literarischen Rhetorik*, 2d ed. [Munich, 1973], p. 361, n. 1. The author gathers the examples of what we call chiasmus under "commutatio" (pp. 395–97). Examples of this figure are, for instance, *in otio tumultuaris in tumultu es otiosus, in re frigidissima cales, in ferventissima friges*, etc. One can see in these examples that the syntactical function (x, y) of the terms a, b is inverted:

$$a^x \, b^y \, b^x \, a^y$$

The syntactical function separates and distinguishes a from a and b from b insuring that the antithesis does not repeat the pairs $a \, b$ and $b \, a$ tautologically.

In Hesiod such syntactical function does not operate: a, b and b, a, therefore, if superimposed, represent a tautology marked only by the inversion and by the different rhetorical emphasis, that the inversion produces.

13.   L. H. Jefferey, *The Local Scripts of Archaic Greece* (Oxford, 1961), pp. 90 ff.: "Perhaps the most interesting archaic inscriptions from Boeotia are those on the relics of bronze tripods or plain *lebetes*, the customary prizes offered at funeral games in early Greece. Hesiod, having won his tripod in the funeral games of Amphidamas at Chalcis, dedicated it in a sanctuary of the Muses (and Helikonios?) on Helikon, where a fragment from the rim of an archaic bronze *lebes* has in fact been found, with part of the dedicatory inscription."

14.   See H. Lansberg, *Handbuch*, p. 361.

15.   On the influence Hesiod exercised in classical culture, see *Hésiode et son influence*, Fondation Hardt, Entretiens sur l'antiquité classique, vol. 7 (Vandoeuvres-Genève, 1962).

Appendix
WRITING

Our analysis has considered the problem of difference within the figurative, metaphorical language of Hesiod—such notions and images as Discord and imitation. In doing so we have respected the conceptual tenets of Hesiod's text. But language clearly does not imitate things: language is a structure of differences and involves a movement of deferral that embraces the whole "sign," i.e., "signifier" and "signified," as our analysis has also shown.

It would therefore be interesting to focus on the signifier itself, which in epic poetry has conspicuous characteristics and unique qualities. Yet the scope of this book does not permit me to undertake such a project at this time. I must limit myself, therefore, to touching upon some of the problems, though I am aware of the general and provisional formulation of my remarks.

The Muses define poetic language as either being truthful or seeming truthful: their implication is that the language of the poets (λέγειν) *always* rings truthful, even when it is not. Their statement, therefore, plays on a special quality, a privileged nature of poetic language. Indeed it is easy, though insufficient, to explain their claim at the level of subject-matter: the events about which the epic poet sings derive from a special memory, since they are either buried in a remote past or hidden in a distant future. The audience has no referent by which to judge the truth of the poetic narrative, and therefore is forced to accept its claims of truthfulness.

But the same conditions function at the level of the "signifier": diction, style, musical and metrical composition—everything in the "signifier" derives from a special memory; the audience's everyday language does not constitute any workable reference since the epic language is an independent linguistic system, handed down by tradition. The language of Homer and Hesiod is an artificial language in the sense that it is traditional: the poets have drawn their

138

modes of speaking not from the language of their time but primarily from a fixed patrimony of lines of poetic texts. These traditional texts are either merely reproduced and re-elaborated, or they function as an independent linguistic system on which the poets build their texts (see M. Durante, *Sulla preistoria della tradizione poetica greca*, [Rome, 1971], p. 20).

This point involves some precise consequences. First, the "signifier," lacking the quality of everydayness, looks consonant with its "signified," which is itself removed from any everyday experience; this creates an illusion of identity. This phenomenon occurs in various degrees in all types of poetic language, but it is certainly conspicuous and remarkable in Greek epic language. (One should not exaggerate, even when dealing with Greek epic, the importance of the remoteness of the subject matter, for if the events themselves are buried in a distant past, the ethos through which the narrator views them is necessarily more contemporary.)

Furthermore, the particular *formulaic* character of the Greek epic strengthens the illusion of its identity, for it creates the sense that this language repeats itself with a consistency unknown to everyday language. Though we know today that the formula does not obey an absolute, economical principle, it is nevertheless generally true that in a given metrical portion, one formulaic "signified" is represented by one, and only one, formula.

No wonder, then, that the language of the Muses always seems truthful: it appears to realize in its own signifier the conditions of the metaphysics of identity that we have outlined. Just as the myth inscribes the difference in the mode of the absence, so the traditional poetic diction seems to write off at least some conspicuous aspects of the differential nature of the signifier itself and to eliminate the difference between signifier and signified. Accordingly it seems able to guarantee a truthful, unchangeable, univocal repetition of the things as they are.

This explanation does not annul the commonly held view that formulaic diction, as a memory aid, is the condition of the success of the oral performance; rather, it complements that view.

Yet the remoteness of epic dialect from everyday language, and its continuous identity, is only relative: the epic language shows in its layers prosodic, grammatical, lexical, and stylistic changes that indicate a long history of modifications. The formulaic diction appears today to be much less pervasive than it appeared to its discoverer; the endless work of adaptation of the *formulae*, in different contexts and after general linguistic modification, introduced remarkable differences in the repetition itself.

The epic language therefore fails to preserve what I would call the mythical condition of its identity and continuity. The signifier, even when it points to the same traditional signified, drifts, in the course of history, to the point that different *formulae* may struggle for the same referent.

A peculiar contradiction, furthermore, threatens the self identity of epic language: because of the oral composition, and because of the unique climate of each performance, the poet is necessarily unable—whatever he may think— to reproduce his composition exactly from one performance to another. Thus, while the epic tradition as a whole shows an astonishing degree of fixity, for an individual text to be fixed in the sense that a written text is fixed is unthinkable. Only writing can insure the permanence and the unalterability of each "performance."

From this point of view, then, what does Hesiod's text teach us? It seems to me that Hesiod's text obeys the conditions created by writing: there is some reason to believe that the text of the *Theogony*, for instance, was written down as soon as it was composed. To be sure, this does not imply that Hesiod composed his texts as a writer does; but my impression is that the experience of writing affected his composition.[1]

The evidence for the first point could be derived by the survival, in the *Theogony*, of versions that Hesiod either changed or expanded in the *Erga*. As we read the Prometheus-Pandora episode in the *Erga*, we realize that the Prometheus story summarizes the long version of the *Theogony*, while the Pandora story expands the version of the *Theogony*. The Prometheus story of the *Erga* appears to have been composed with the text of the *Theogony* in mind: through an appropriate repetition of some lines, the poet alludes to his previous version, while leaving the story as a whole unchanged.[2]

Now let us assume that the "oral composer," Hesiod, sings his *Theogony* sometime after he has already composed the *Erga*. It is reasonable to suppose that he would not leave a painstakingly composed, more recent version of the Pandora episode totally unused. It is difficult to believe that he would simply forget his recasting of the episode, the bewildering story of the jar, his bitterer view of the human "beginning." Using the oral technique, he would easily add some of the *Erga* episodes to his new singing of the *Theogony*; he would try a more or less felicitious addition of the old material to the new, even so discreet an addition as the name Pandora and the story of the jar. Had he made such additions several times, little by little the two versions would have become more and more similar. But our text of the *Theogony* shows no trace of this speculated process. We should then conclude that for Hesiod, the text of the *Theogony* was *unalterable*, once composed. Hesiod must have felt that the text could not be changed, but must be sung exactly as he had composed it, even if he eventually composed better versions of the same story himself. Whether it was written down or firmly entrusted to an unfaltering memory, he treasured his text as a property with an unalterable form.

The pecularity of treasuring a text as unalterable may not necessarily imply writing, since the epic language seems characterized by this same tendency, and since the poets apparently believed that they were repeating exactly what they knew or had heard; but the fact that the text of the *Theogony* has reached us unaffected by Hesiod's subsequent additions to the myth of Prometheus and Pandora should indicate that it was written down—or never repeated—once composed and performed.

The same conclusions might be drawn by the palinode that Hesiod writes in the *Erga*, when he asserts that there are two Discords (11 ff.). If Hesiod had not considered the text of the *Theogony* unalterable, he could have easily introduced a few lines after *Theogony* 232 saying that there is also a good Eris, mother of Zelos (emulation) and of Kotos (anger). Parenthetically, we might wonder whether Hesiod, if he were invited to produce the *Theogony* after his palinode, would still repeat that there is only one Eris, persistently evil and mother of evils. I find this hard to believe; and, given the premise that Hesiod considered his text unalterable, the conclusion must be that after the composition of the *Erga*, he would not sing the *Theogony*. Even more radical would be the conclusion that his compositions were prepared for one or more special occasions, and not for regular performance. But, in principle, one cannot reject the possibility that even after the composition of the *Erga*, if invited to sing the *Theogony*, he would have sung it as it has come to us, with the old version of Eris.

Let us now turn to the moment of composition of the new version of Eris. On the one hand, the old text is obsolete, since it contains only a part of the truth; on the other, it constitutes the model for the poet's re-elaboration. Notice that the poet does not need to repeat the genealogy of the bad Eris: he introduces only that of the good Eris (line 17) saying that she was born earlier (προτέρην) of Night. He adapts the new text to the old one smoothly and corrects it.

Here we have something more than the evidence for the unalterability of the *Theogony* text: we have a hint as to a mode of composition that presumes that Hesiod "read" his previous text. For only a careful reading of the old text and writing of the new will insure the success of a recantation, its precise limits, and its adaptation to the old text. Examples abound of compositions that carefully allude to precise Homeric phrases and look like mosaics. In *Erga* 62-63, for instance, three Homeric lines are re-elaborated, both to preserve formulaic diction and to allude to Helen: small changes, such as the dative plural in —ης (which is rarely used in Homer: see Chantraine, *Grammaire homérique*, vol. 1, p. 202) and ἐίσκειν instead of ἐοίκεν insure the adaptation. To be sure, the text sounds at least redundant, but only because it is too rich in suggestions. This mode of composition, however successful, seems to me to differ slightly from the written one: a careful reading and writing insure the possibility of precise allusions, of a subtle combination of expressions, of smooth changes and variations.

The breath of the Muses (*Th.* 31) becomes "text" through this process and becomes unalterable by being written down. Writing was certainly emerging in Hesiod's time: together with trade, crafts, and the crisis of agriculture, it was to fashion a new world. As competition, trade, emigrations, and colonization were carrying Greeks far across the sea, so writing, in a Platonic image, was to move them out of themselves and out of mythical truth.

NOTES

1.   The question of whether Hesiod wrote his text is a complex and much-debated problem. See West, Prolegomena, pp. 40–48: he presents strong stylistical arguments suggesting "painful written rather than unencumbered oral creation" (p. 40).

2.   In the new, abridged version of the Prometheus story, the poet takes special care to record Prometheus's theft of fire, because this gesture provokes Zeus's decision to create the woman (*Th.* 570; *Erga* 57). The repetition of a similar expression in these two lines constitutes a sort of seal authenticating the parallelism of the two versions. In the *Erga* Hesiod leaves aside the theme of the division of the meat—probably because it was too long for the new text—but he adds the motive of the concealment of the livelihood and makes more explicit from the beginning the sense of fall and loss implicit in the quarrel initiated between Zeus and Prometheus (43–46). See Fink, "Pandora und Epimetheus" (Ph.D. diss., Erlangen, 1958), p. 56.

SELECTED BIBLIOGRAPHY

Becker, O. *Das Bild des Weges.* Berlin, 1937.

Benveniste, E. *Le vocabulaire des institutions indo-européennes.* 2 vols. Paris, 1967. English Translation: *Indo-European Language and Society*, Miami, Fla., 1971.

Bona Quaglia, L. *Gli "Erga" di Esiodo.* Turin, 1973.

Chantraine, P. *Dictionnaire étymologique de la langue grecque.* Paris, 1967 ff.

_____. *Grammaire homérique.* 2 vols. Paris, 1958, 1963.

Detienne, M. *Crise agraire et attitude religieuse chez Hésiode.* Collection "Latomus", vol 68. Brussels-Berchem, 1963.

_____. *Les maîtres de vérité dans la Grèce archaïque.* Paris, 1967.

Edwards, G. P. *The Language of Hesiod in Its Traditional Context.* Oxford, 1971.

Ehrenberg, V. *Die Rechtsidee im frühen Griechentum.* Leipzig, 1921.

Lain Entralgo, P. *The Therapy of the Word in Classical Antiquity.* New Haven, 1970.

Evelyn-White, H. G. *Hesiod. The Homeric Hymns and Homerica.* Loeb Classical Library. London and Cambridge (Mass.), 1967.

Fink, G. "Pandora and Epimetheus". Ph.D. dissertation, Erlangen, 1958.

Frisk, H. F. *Griechisches etymologisches Wörterbuch.* 2 vols. Heidelberg, 1960.

Groningen, B. A., van. "Hésiode et Persès." *Mededelingen der Koninklijke Nederlandse Akademie van Wetenschappen, Afd. Letterkunde.* Nieuwe Reeks, Deel 20, n. 6 (1957).

Hays, H. M. *Notes on the "Works and Days" of Hesiod.* Chicago, 1918.

Heitsch, E. "Das Prometheus-Gedicht bei Hesiod." *Rheinisches Museum* 1963: 1–15.

Hesiod. *Theogony.* Edited, with prolegomena and commentary, by M. L. West. Oxford, 1966.

Hesiod. *Opera et Dies.* Recensuit A. Colonna. Milan, 1959.

Hommel, H. "Wahrheit und Gerechtigkeit." *Antike und Abendland* 15 (1969): 159 ff.

Krafft, F. *Vergleichende Untersuchungen zu Homer und Hesiod.* Göttingen, 1963.

Lendle, O. *Die 'Pandorasage' bei Hesiod: Textkritische und Motivgeschichtliche Untersuchungen.* Wurzburg, 1957.

Leumann, M. *Homerische Wörter.* Basel, 1950.

Luther, W. "Wahrheit Licht und Erkenntniss in der Griechische Philosophie bis Demokrit." *Archiv für Begriffsgeschichte* 10 (1966): 1–240.

Mazon, P. *Hésiode, "Le Travaux et les Jours."* Paris, 1914.

Nagy, G. *Comparative Studies in Greek and Indic Meter.* Cambridge, Mass., 1974.

Nicolai, W. *Hesiods Erga: Beobachtungen zum Aufbau.* Heidelberg, 1964.

Pagliaro, A. "Aedi e rapsodi" in *Saggi di critica semantica.* Messina and Florence, 1953.

Pertusi, A. *Scholia Vetera in Hesiodi "Opera et dies."* Milan, 1955.

Puelma, M. "Sänger und König. Zum Verständnis von Hesiods Tierfabel." *Museum Helveticum* 29, (1972): 86–109

Robert, C. "Pandora." *Hermes* 49 (1914): 17–38.

Rzach, A. *Hesiodi Carmina* (editio maior). Leipzig, 1902.

Schwyzer, E. *Griechische Grammatik.* 2 vols. Munich, 1939.

Sellschopp, I. *Stilistische Untersuchungen zu Hesiod.* Hamburg, 1934.

Sinclair, T. A. *Hesiod's "Works and Days."* London, 1932.

Solmsen, F. *Hesiod and Aeschylus.* Ithaca, N.Y., 1949.

————. *Hesiodi: Theogonia, Opera et Dies, Scutum.* Oxford, 1970.

Vernant, J. P. "Le mythe hésiodique des races. Essai d'analyse structurale." *Revue d'histoire des religions* 157 (1960): 21–56.

————. "Le mythe hésiodique des races. Sur un essai de mise au point." *Revue de Philologie* ser. 3, 40 (1966): 247–76.

Welskopf, E. C. *Probleme der Musse im alten Hellas.* Berlin, 1962.

Wilamowitz-Moellendorff, U., von. *Hesiodos Erga.* Berlin, 1928.

Wolf, E. *Griechisches Rechtsdenken.* 2 vols. Frankfort, 1950.

Index of Names and Notions

Numbers in italic type refer to the Greek texts.

Library of Congress Cataloging in Publication Data

Pucci, Pietro.
    Hesiod and the language of poetry.

    Bibliography: p. 143
    Includes index.
    1.   Hesiodus–Criticism and interpretation.   I.   Title.
PA4011.P8   881'.01   76-234
ISBN 0-8018-1787-0